RIBSY

RIBSY

BEVERLY CLEARY

ILLUSTRATED BY
LOUIS DARLING

HOUGHTON MIFFLIN COMPANY

BOSTON

Atlanta   Dallas   Geneva, Illinois
Palo Alto   Princeton   Toronto

Houghton Mifflin Edition, 1993

Printed in the U.S.A.

ISBN 0-395-61791-X

456789-B-96 95 94 93

Contents

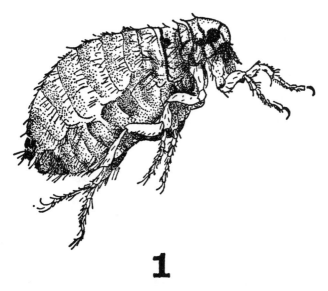

1

Ribsy and the Hungry Flea

HENRY HUGGINS' dog Ribsy was a plain ordinary city dog, the kind of dog that strangers usually called Mutt or Pooch. They always called him this in a friendly way, because Ribsy was a friendly dog. He followed Henry and his friends to school. He kept the mailman company. He wagged his tail at the milkman, who always stopped to pet him. People liked Ribsy, and Ribsy liked people. Ribsy was what you might call a well-adjusted dog.

This did not mean that Ribsy had no troubles. He did have troubles, and high on the list were fleas, particularly one mean hungry flea that persistently nipped Ribsy right under his collar where he could not get at it no matter how hard he scratched with his hind foot. If it had not been for that flea, things might have been different for Ribsy.

Ribsy's troubles began one Saturday morning in October when he was sitting out in front of the Huggins' square white house on Klickitat Street keeping an eye on the brand-new station wagon to make sure the family did not drive away without him. The Hugginses had owned the new green station wagon almost a week, and not once had Ribsy been allowed to ride in it.

"We're going to keep this car clean," vowed Mrs. Huggins. "No more muddy paw prints on the seats. No more smudgy nose marks on the windows."

Ribsy knew the Hugginses were getting ready to go someplace, because he could hear Mrs. Huggins tapping around in high heels, a sure sign that she was about to leave the house. He had also sensed an air of hurry that morning. Henry had dumped half a can of Woofies Dog Food on Ribsy's dish without stopping to scratch him behind the ears. Nosy the cat had been fed and hurriedly shoved outdoors. The Hugginses had not lingered at the breakfast table. All this meant the family was going someplace, and this time Ribsy did not intend to be left behind.

While Ribsy kept an eye on the station wagon he amused himself with his soggy old tennis ball, wet from last night's rain, which he dropped at the top of the driveway and caught as it rolled to the bottom. Then he sat down and, with a great jingling of license tags, scratched. He dug in with the toenails of his left hind foot, starting under his chin and gradually twisting his head until he was scratching the back of his neck. Then he switched to his right hind foot and scratched the other half of his neck. All this scratching did no good, because his collar got in the way of his toenails. He still itched. The mean hungry flea knew exactly the spots that Ribsy could not reach.

Henry came out of the house wearing his raincoat and helmet. He stopped to pat Ribsy on the head. Then he scratched his dog behind the ears at the point where the hair became soft and silky. "Want to play catch?" he asked, picking up the ball and throwing it across the lawn.

Ribsy caught the ball on the first bounce and dropped it at Henry's feet before he had to sit down and scratch again. That flea was driving him crazy.

Henry's friend Beezus, whose real name was Beatrice, and her little sister Ramona came running down the street. "Can you go to the park?" Beezus asked Henry. "Mother said we have to get out of the house awhile before it starts raining again."

"Nope," said Henry, picking up the tennis ball. "We're going down to the shopping center to buy some paint and new jeans and a bunch of stuff."

Beezus held out her hand to Ribsy. "Shake hands," she said. Ribsy agreeably held out his left paw and allowed the girl to shake it. "Isn't he ever going to learn to use his right hand—I mean paw?" asked Beezus.

"There are left-handed people. Why shouldn't there be left-pawed dogs?" This seemed reasonable to Henry.

Ramona ran to Ribsy, dropped to her knees even though the ground was wet, and threw her arms around his neck good and tight. Ribsy knew what to do about a small girl like Ramona. Patience was the answer. Just stand still long enough and she would go away. It sometimes took quite a bit of patience to get rid of Ramona.

She pressed her face against his and said,

"Don't I look cute? Daddy ought to get a picture of this."

"Oh, Ramona," said Beezus crossly. "Daddy can't take a picture of everything you do. Come on. Stop choking Ribsy, and let's go to the park."

Patience had worked. Ribsy was free of Ramona.

"So long," said Henry to Beezus, as his mother and father came out of the house and climbed into the front seat of the station wagon. Henry threw the ball down the street and started to climb in after them. This time Ribsy did not chase his ball, which he knew was perfectly safe lying in the gutter. No one ever bothered his soggy old ball no matter where he left it.

When Ribsy was a few feet from the station wagon, the mean hungry flea gave him an extra-hard nip. Ribsy could not stand it. He had to sit down for one quick scratch.

"Henry, don't let that dog in this car," said Mrs. Huggins.

Henry hopped in and slammed the door.

"Sorry, old boy," he said to his dog, who had finished scratching and was wagging his tail.

The car started and Ribsy was left behind. Ribsy was not a dog to give up easily. He could be almost as persistent as his flea, and now he started running down the street as fast as he could after his family's new car. This had happened before with the old car, and he knew that by running fast he could catch up at the first stop sign. He managed to stay close enough to get thoroughly drenched with muddy water when the car drove through a puddle. As he expected, he made it to the stop sign, where he stood panting and looking hopefully at his family.

Henry pushed the button that lowered the window. "Ribsy! Go home!" he called out.

Ribsy answered with a short, sharp bark that meant, No, I don't want to go home. When the car started up, he continued his chase. Water spattered as the tires sucked at the pavement. He caught up at the second stop sign, three blocks away.

"Wuf!" said Ribsy, wagging his tail. For a middle-aged dog Ribsy could run pretty fast.

"Ribsy, go home!" said Henry, speaking less sharply this time.

"Don't pay any attention to him," said Mrs. Huggins. "Just ignore him, and he'll go home when he gets tired."

"That dog can run twenty miles an hour," said Mr. Huggins, who had been clocking Ribsy with the speedometer.

As the car started, Ribsy gathered all his strength and, even though he was getting tired and that flea was chewing away under his collar, he managed to catch up at the third stop sign.

"Don't even look at him," said Mrs. Huggins. "Just pretend he isn't there."

"Aw, Mom," protested Henry. "He's getting tired. He's panting so he can't even bark."

"Good," said Mrs. Huggins, who was usually a kind woman. "Now maybe he'll go home. He's not going to ride in our clean new car."

Mr. Huggins went on, and so did Ribsy, his

tongue flapping like a flag and his feet scissoring back and forth as fast as he could make them go. Henry's worried face watched him from the tail gate of the station wagon. Ribsy barely made it to the next stop, which was a traffic light at a busy intersection. He stood panting with his sides going in and out like bellows.

"But Mom, he'll get run over," Henry was saying. "He wants to come with us so much he isn't even paying any attention to the other cars."

Mrs. Huggins glanced unwillingly at Ribsy. "Oh, all right," she said. "Just this once. But keep him on the floor. I don't want him on the seat with those wet paws, and I don't want any smeary nose prints on the windows."

Henry opened the door, and Ribsy, the winner, jumped in. The first thing he did was shake himself. Muddy drops splattered over the new plastic upholstery. Silently Mrs. Huggins handed Henry a Kleenex, and without a word he wiped the spatters. Until Ribsy had caught his breath he was satisfied to stay on the floor, even though he did not like the strong smell of the new car. As soon as he was breathing normally he tried to climb on the seat, where the smell was not so strong, and where he could ride with his nose out the window and smell more things faster.

"No, Ribsy," said Henry, shoving his dog off the seat. "Down, boy."

And so Ribsy was forced to ride on the floor of the station wagon. He could not see a thing, and the new-car smell—a mixture of new rubber, plastic floor matting, and lubricating oil—was strong. Ribsy did not like it. He preferred the odors of wet earth, fallen leaves, cats, food cooking, and boys, particularly his own boy, Henry Huggins. However, Ribsy was a dog who always tried to make the best of things, and this was a good chance to scratch again. He began under his chin with his left hind foot, and finished on the other side with his right foot, but no matter how hard he scratched, no matter how hard he jingled his license tags, he could not reach the bites under his collar.

Henry Huggins was the kind of boy who understood. "Here, let me help," he said, and removed Ribsy's collar.

Ribsy enjoyed a good hard scratch, this time one that really did some good. When he had finished, he laid his chin on Henry's knee. He was filled with love and gratitude for Henry's kindness. He loved Henry more than anyone in the world.

Henry understood. He rubbed Ribsy behind the ear. "Good old Ribsy," he said affectionately. "Did you think I wanted to leave you behind?"

By this time the Hugginses had reached the shopping center, which was made up of all kinds of stores, shops, and restaurants, surrounded by acres and acres of parking space without parking meters. People came from miles around to shop here, because they did not have to worry about finding a parking space, and they could shop as long as they wished without having to remember the time and rush out to put another nickel in a meter.

"You stay here, Ribsy," said Henry. He carefully opened two of the windows a few inches at the top, so Ribsy would have plenty of air while he was locked in the car. It took Henry longer than usual to adjust the windows, which worked automatically and were fun to play with. Just push a button, and zip, they went up. Push it again, and zip, they went down.

For once Ribsy did not mind being left in the car, and as soon as the Hugginses had disappeared in the acres of parking spaces on their way to the stores, he jumped up on one of the seats, blissfully scratched his collar-free neck, turned around three times, settled his nose on his tail, and went to sleep. He slept quite awhile, and when he awoke he felt rested and ready for action. Unfortunately, there was not much opportunity for action locked in a station wagon, and Ribsy had to content himself by pressing his damp nose against the clean windows while he watched people walking across the parking lot. Sometimes they spoke to him. "Hi there, Pooch," or, "Hello, Mutt," a person would say, and Ribsy would answer with a short bark and a wag of his tail, to show he was a sociable dog who would rather be out running around instead of being shut up in this new-smelling car.

Ribsy tolerated his imprisonment until a little Pomeranian happened to come along on the end

of a leash. It was a silly little dog that took one look at Ribsy and began to yap.

Something about the little dog annoyed Ribsy. He barked good and loud, to let it know that he was bigger and stronger and did not care to be yapped at. He was not always as friendly with dogs as he was with people.

The Pomeranian knew that Ribsy could not get out and that he was safe. He yapped harder in a way that said quite plainly, Ha-ha, you can't catch me.

"Come along, Fluffy," said the lady on the other end of the Pomeranian's leash. "I won't let the bad dog hurt you."

The little dog was having such a good time barking at a bigger dog who could not get at him that he stood his ground and yapped harder. *Yap-yap-yap. Yap-yap-yap.*

This infuriated Ribsy. He clawed at the glass and poked his nose out the opening at the top to bark back. No dog that size could talk to him like that and get away with it.

"Come *on,* Fluffy." The lady pulled at the leash.

Fluffy did not want to go, and so his owner was forced to pick him up and carry him. The little dog looked over his mistress's shoulder and went right on yapping at Ribsy as he was carried off down the lane between two rows of parked cars.

This made Ribsy frantic to escape. Barking wildly, he scrabbled his paws against the door of the station wagon. In doing so, he hit the button that controlled the automatic window. The glass slid down, and Ribsy leaped through the window to the wet pavement. It all happened so fast that he was still surprised when his feet hit the ground, but he lost no time in dashing off in the direction in which the little dog and his owner had gone. He followed the sound of the yapping as it went toward the stores, but when it stopped he quickly lost interest.

After sitting down to have another good scratch at his collar-free neck, Ribsy set out to find Henry Huggins, who had disappeared someplace in the sea of cars. He put his nose down to the pavement and began to sniff. He was searching for a certain familiar scent, a scent that was made up of a number of things—sneakers, raincoat, a whiff of cat, the aroma of coffee grounds that had been spilled on the kitchen floor that morning, the smell of the new car, and, most satisfying of all to Ribsy, the boy smell that belonged only to Henry Huggins.

Ribsy had a pretty good nose, but unfortunately he was no bloodhound. He had never tracked a lost child over mountains and through forests. He was just an ordinary city dog, trying to track his owner across an enormous parking lot that smelled of oil and exhaust. As Ribsy ran whiffling around the parking lot, his nose picked up the scents of many pairs of shoes and quite a few pairs of galoshes, some of them tinged with the smell of cat and many of them smelling of boy, but none of them smelling of Henry.

When he had worked his way to the stores and shops, he found all sorts of interesting smells that were not on the ground. There were popcorn and new shoe leather and hamburgers frying. Ribsy took a great interest in the hamburgers and sat for quite a while by the door of the coffee shop, but no one suggested that he go in.

A pet shop was interesting, too, because one of the windows was full of puppies, tumbling about on shredded newspaper. Ribsy put his paws up on the front of the shop and barked at the puppies, who stopped rolling around and barked back in their shrill little voices. This dialogue between the middle-aged dog and the puppies attracted a crowd, but Henry and his parents were not part of it. After a while Ribsy tired of the puppies, who were silly young things, and wandered on, exploring and looking for Henry when he thought of it.

Rain was falling hard now, but Ribsy was dry, because there were roofs over the sidewalks of the shopping center. The harder the rain fell, the faster people hurried toward their cars. A feeling of uneasiness came over Ribsy. He was looking for someone, and it was time he found him. Down went his nose to the pavement, and he whiffled his way out into the rain, searching in earnest along the black asphalt, painted with diagonal white lines that marked the parking spaces.

Ribsy ran every which way, trying to pick up the familiar scent. Cars honked at him. The rain, which pelted his skin with cold hard drops, turned the pavement into one big muddle of smells, mostly oil, gasoline, and exhaust. Ribsy was worried. Nothing was familiar. When a car slammed on its brakes to avoid hitting him, he became frantic. The car honked angrily, and its chrome shone menacingly.

"Watch where you're going, you stupid mutt," the driver bawled.

Ribsy began to run. He ran as fast as he could,

dodging in and out among the acres of parked cars in the direction from which he thought he had come. He could find no landmarks. All the white stripes on the asphalt were exactly alike, and all the cars looked pretty much the same to Ribsy. No matter which way he ran there were more cars and more white lines. He was confused, bewildered, and frightened. He was also sopping wet.

And then Ribsy caught a familiar scent. Even

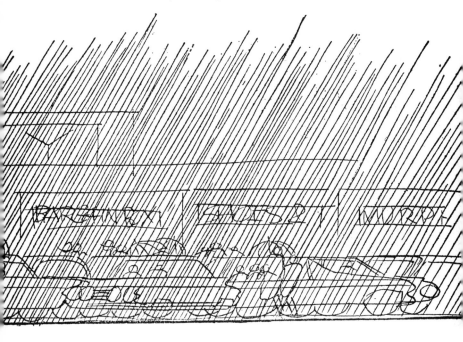

in the rain it was clear and unmistakable. It was the smell of a new car, and it was right beside him. There in the next lane was a blue station wagon that smelled just right. Ribsy, who like all dogs was color-blind, investigated. He found the tail-gate window open, and with a leap and a scramble he was inside where it was dry. After giving himself a good hard shake that sent off a shower of rainwater, he curled up on a seat in the smallest possible space to try to warm himself. There he fell asleep while he waited for his family to come back.

It was some time later that Ribsy was awakened by a man's voice, saying, "I thought I told you girls not to play around these windows."

Suddenly the car seemed to be full of people, most of them girls, dressed in raincoats, corduroy slacks, and boots. Bewildered and half-awake, Ribsy sat up.

"Daddy, look! A dog!" cried the oldest girl, who was about Henry Huggins' age.

"Well, where did you come from?" asked the father, addressing Ribsy.

"I *thought* something smelled peculiar," said the mother. "It was wet dog."

"Can we keep him?" asked the second oldest girl, whose raincoat had been mended with adhesive tape.

"Of course not," said the mother. "Open the door and let him out."

A chorus of protest arose from the children. "*Please* let us keep him!" "He's such a *nice* dog!" "We need a dog."

"*Open the door and let him out,*" repeated the father above the din. "He looks well-fed. He obviously belongs to someone."

"But he isn't wearing a collar," the oldest girl pointed out.

"Zibby, *open the door and let him out.*" Zibby opened the door. Ribsy realized that something had gone wrong somehow, but he was reluctant to leave the familiar smell.

"Give him a shove," said the father.

Zibby shoved Ribsy, but she shoved gently.

Ribsy hopped out into the rain, and the door was slammed behind him. He stood shivering, and looked hopefully at the car as if he somehow expected this family to turn into the Huggins family.

The people in the car stared back. Ribsy started to walk away, stopped, and looked back. It was all so puzzling. The car smelled right, but the people were wrong.

"He's lost," said Zibby. "He's lost and he's cold. Daddy, we can't just leave him there."

A chorus of agreement arose from the rest of the children. "We can't just leave him there."

"We could take him to the Lost and Found," said one of the younger girls, the one in the peaked hood.

"Silly, stores don't have a Lost and Found for dogs, just for mittens and things like that." Zibby was inclined to act a little superior. She was also bossy. "Can't we take him home and look in the paper and see if somebody advertises for him?"

"Well. . . ." The mother was the kind of person who did not like to discourage her children's ideas. She wanted them to develop initiative. Besides, a dog might amuse them on a long wet afternoon when they had to be cooped up in the house. "Perhaps we shouldn't leave him here on the parking lot. He might get hit by a car."

"Maybe he won't come," said the father. "I hope."

Zibby opened the door. "Here, doggie," she invited.

Ribsy stood watching uncertainly. The girl hopped out, grabbed him around the middle, and lugged him back to the station wagon, where she dumped him on the seat beside the next-to-the-oldest girl.

"Maybe we'll get a reward for finding him," said the next-to-the-oldest.

"Maybe a million dollars," said the next-to-the-youngest.

"Nobody will give a million dollars for a dog," said Zibby. "Anyway, I hope nobody advertises for him, so we can keep him."

"Maybe we'll advertise him ourselves," said the father, as he started the car and drove away. "Found: one mutt, in parking lot."

Ribsy whimpered uneasily. Many hands of different sizes were petting him all at once, and although he did not dislike small girls, he had learned to be cautious around them. They might turn out to be like Ramona, hugging him, petting him too hard, pulling his tail.

"Oh where, oh where, has my little dog gone?" the father began to sing as he drove off. All the girls joined in with enthusiasm.

"Oh where, oh where can he be?
With his tail cut short and his ears cut long,
Oh where, oh where can he be?"

Ribsy did not care for singing. But even more than the singing and the many strange hands petting him, Ribsy was bothered by something else. He sensed that the car was going in the wrong direction. It crossed a bridge over a river, passed tall buildings that were not the least bit like Klickitat Street, and took a road uphill through a canyon that led out of the city.

Ribsy scrambled across Zibby's lap and pressed

his nose against the window of the station wagon, where he whimpered anxiously. He was so frightened that his paw pads began to perspire and leave damp footprints on the seat. Everything was wrong. The wrong people were in the new-smelling car. The car was going in the wrong direction, and there was no way that he could escape. His neck still itched, but he scratched half-heartedly. He had more important worries than the flea that had caused him to be without his collar and identifying tags. He was being carried farther and farther away from Henry Huggins, and that, as far as Ribsy was concerned, was the worst thing that could happen to him.

"Oh where, oh where, has my little dog gone?" sang all the little girls at the tops of their voices. "Oh where, oh where can he be?"

"Right here with us," said Zibby happily.

2
The Cleanest Dog
in the U.S.A.

"RIBSY! RIBSY!" Henry and his mother and father had been splashing up and down the aisles of the parking area of the shopping center for almost an hour calling and searching for their dog. Finally they gathered, damp and discouraged, in the new green station wagon.

"He isn't anyplace in this entire parking area," said Mrs. Huggins, sinking wearily back in the front seat.

"Do you suppose somebody stole him?" Henry could not understand Ribsy's disappearance.

"He's not what you would call a valuable dog," said Mrs. Huggins. "He is hardly the kind of dog someone would want to steal."

"I call him a valuable dog," said Henry glumly. "Even if he doesn't have a pedigree." Henry, who did not like to go shopping, was tired and hungry. It seemed to him they had spent hours trudging around the shopping center looking for bargains and more hours slogging around the wet parking lot searching for Ribsy.

"Somehow he must have bumped against the button that made the automatic window go down, and then he jumped out," guessed Mr. Huggins.

Henry brightened. "I know. Ribsy got tired of waiting, so he started home all by himself. I bet he's home right now waiting for us on the doormat." Henry had wanted to start home a long time ago himself. He had wanted to start home as soon as he reached the shopping center. The only reason he had come in the first place was to ride in the new station wagon.

"Let's hope so." Mr. Huggins started the car.

Henry settled back to enjoy the sound of the

new motor—it was so smooth it made their old car sound like a pile of junk. He had nothing to worry about. Ribsy would be waiting at home.

Ribsy, however, was riding in the opposite direction from home in a blue station wagon with a family named Dingley. The Dingley children were called, from the oldest to the youngest, Zibby, Louanne, Sally, Lisa, and George. George was a fat twenty-month-old baby with beautiful golden curls. All five children were busy petting the nice doggie. This was much more fun than petting a stuffed animal.

Ribsy understood that small children, like the puppies in the pet-shop window, were too young to know what they were doing, and so he was patient. He had learned this from long experience with Ramona. Just be patient, and pretty soon they would stop. It took a lot of patience to wait for five children, who had never owned a dog, to tire of petting him.

When at last he was free of all those hands, Ribsy enjoyed a good hard scratch.

"Doggie!" cried George joyfully.

"George can say doggie!" Louanne was proud of her little brother.

"It looks to me as if the doggie has fleas," observed Mrs. Dingley, as the station wagon sped out of the city toward a subdivision of new houses.

Zibby took charge. "We will give him a bath," she announced.

"I would love to help give him a bath," said Louanne. All the girls were delighted with the idea. This had looked like another long rainy Saturday, and now look what had happened. They had a dog to wash.

"In the Bathinette?" asked Lisa.

"No, silly," said Zibby. "In the bathtub. He can't scratch it, because there's a rubber mat on the bottom."

"I don't know about that," said Mr. Dingley, as they turned off the highway onto a side road.

"Oh, I think it would be all right," said Mrs. Dingley, "if they clean out the bathtub afterward." She did not want to discourage her children's initiative. She was also glad they had thought of something that would keep them entertained on the long wet afternoon.

Zibby threw her arms around Ribsy, and said, "I just love the dog, and I hope we get to keep him."

Ribsy, who knew that Zibby was almost as big as Henry Huggins and, therefore, old enough to know what she was doing, wriggled free.

"Don't get your hopes up," said Mr. Dingley. "He's too well-fed to have been lost long. Someone is sure to be looking for him."

The family drove into the double garage of a ranch house under some fir trees. Ribsy jumped out with the children and barely had time to pause by a bush before Zibby grabbed him. "Come on, doggie," she said, picking him up and lugging him into the house. Ribsy struggled. He did not like to be carried.

"Now can we give him a bath?" asked Sally.

"Put your raincoats and boots away first," said Mrs. Dingley. The four little girls ran to their rooms, the older girls to hurl their raincoats and boots on their beds, the younger girls to drop theirs on the floor.

Ribsy trotted nervously from window to window, putting his paws on the sills and whimpering to get out. He had not liked all those little hands petting him, and he felt uneasy in this strange house.

George tottered after Ribsy and seized him by the tail. "Doggie," he said.

"Mother, he said doggie *again*," marveled Louanne. George was such a smart baby.

There was nothing for Ribsy to do but be patient until George tired of his tail. He heard water running in a bathtub, but this did not interest him. He had heard water run into a bathtub often, and knew it had nothing to do with him.

"Maybe we should feed the dog first," suggested Sally.

Zibby had the answer. "You aren't supposed to eat for an hour before going swimming."

"I bet the owner will be glad to get a nice clean dog back," said Louanne.

"Here, doggie," coaxed Zibby.

Ribsy looked questioningly at her and then followed, because he thought she was going to let him out of the house.

"Good doggie," said Zibby, when they reached the bathroom. She seized him around the middle and dumped him into the tub of warm water.

Ribsy was taken completely by surprise. Nothing like this had ever happened to him before. On the rare occasions when Henry Huggins gave him a bath, he used a laundry tub in the basement. Then Ribsy knew what was coming and could hide behind the furnace. Henry always caught him eventually, but Ribsy at least had the fun of a lively chase around the furnace and maybe even up the stairs and through the house if Henry had forgotten to close the basement door.

But this—Ribsy scrambled frantically, trying to get a toehold. Water splashed all over the row of four little girls, who screamed with delight and would not let him out of the tub. Ribsy barked to tell them he did not like this one bit.

George toddled into the bathroom. "Doggie?" he inquired. "Doggie?"

"He says doggie all the time," marveled Louanne, wiping water out of her eyes with her sleeve.

Ribsy gave up the struggle. Once more patience had to be the answer. He simply stood, his head and tail drooping, waiting for this miserable adventure to end so that he could escape.

"Where's the soap?" demanded Zibby. "Somebody get me the soap."

Sally handed her a cake of soap from the washbasin, and the four girls took their washcloths and went to work. Their efforts made Ribsy even more miserable. He was sad and he was soggy. Then two fat little hands, one of them clutching a plastic bottle, pushed between the girls. Crowing with delight at his own cleverness, George emptied an entire bottle of violet-scented bubble bath over Ribsy.

"George!" cried Louanne. "Not the whole bottle!"

"Bubble bath!" Joyfully Sally and Lisa began to swish their hands in the water to make bubbles, lots of them. Giving a dog a bath was fun, but giving a dog a bubble bath was even more fun. Eight hands and a whole bottle of bubble-bath can make a lot of bubbles. The girls screamed with pleasure as Ribsy found himself surrounded by billows of bubbles that were rising higher and higher.

The white tub, the screaming girls, the foaming stuff were all too much for Ribsy. He was through with patience, and he was getting out of

here. With one tremendous effort, he sprang out of the tub, pushing his way between two of the girls, and raced frantically down the hall, trailing water and bubbles behind him. Unfortunately, he did not know where to go, so he raced through the living room and into the kitchen, into the dining room and back to the living room, where he started all over again with the four little girls, followed by their mother and father, running after him. Around and around they went, until at last he found some refuge among the legs of the chairs under the dining-room table.

There, trying to shake off the hateful, smelly stuff, Ribsy sent drops of water and bits of foam flying in all directions.

"Oh dear," said Mrs. Dingley, realizing that she had made a mistake in encouraging quite so much initiative.

Ribsy barked at the Dingleys through the chair legs.

"How are we going to rinse him?" wailed Louanne.

Ribsy barked harder.

"We can't leave the poor thing covered with bubble bath," agreed Mrs. Dingley, who was remarkably calm under the circumstances. With five children and a wet dog in the house on a rainy day she had to stay calm.

"George did it," said Lisa, who was often blamed when things went wrong. "He wasted a whole bottle of bubble bath."

"Tattletale." Louanne always defended her little brother.

It was time for Mr. Dingley to take charge. "Zibby, let the water out of the tub and fill it with fresh water," he directed. "Louanne, see if you can find some old bath towels." While he gave orders he was pulling the chairs away from the table.

Before the last chair was removed Ribsy made a dash for freedom, only to discover he still had the same problem. There was no place to dash to. The kitchen and living room had not helped before, so this time he ran down the hall and tried a different room. It was a bedroom, and he promptly crawled under a bed, way back as far as he could go. It was dusty, and between the fluffs of dust and the perfume of the bubble bath Ribsy sneezed. He sneezed a second time, and was beginning to feel chilly after the warm water. By now he was too miserable to bark or even to whimper.

"He's catching cold." Louanne was on her hands and knees peering under the bedspread at Ribsy, huddled in the corner.

The rest of the family got on their hands and knees, too, and there was Ribsy hemmed in by a row of faces.

"Do you think he'll bite?" asked Sally, the worrier of the family.

"I don't think so," said Mr. Dingley. "He looks like a pretty good-natured dog to me."

Ribsy did not bite people. Once in a while he might try to bite another dog who provoked him, but not people. He was not angry. He was baffled. He could not understand the smelly stuff that foamed all over him. It did not hurt. When he tried to bite it, all he got was an unpleasant taste in his mouth.

"Get some hamburger," ordered Mr. Dingley. "Maybe we can coax him out."

Mrs. Dingley left the room and returned with a lamb chop, which she handed to her husband. "We're out of hamburger," she explained. "The girls ate it all last night."

Mr. Dingley held the chop out to Ribsy. "Nice doggie," he coaxed. "Come and get it."

Ribsy did not care for the lamb chop. In all the excitement he had lost his appetite. Besides, he was cold.

"Look, he's shivering," reported Louanne.

"We'll have to move the bed," said her father. "Get ready, everybody, to catch him in case he makes a dash for it." Then he pulled the bed away from the wall.

Ribsy did not appear. He moved with the bed, and this time he crawled to the center. He did not intend to come out while all those people were there.

"I'll get the dust mop," said Mrs. Dingley.

The dust mop did it. Ribsy did not like being poked with that fuzzy thing, so he backed away.

"I've got him!" Zibby was triumphant as she grabbed Ribsy by the hind legs.

"Come on, boy," said Mr. Dingley gently, as he took hold of Ribsy's hind legs and dragged him out from under the bed. Ribsy, who now had fluffs of dust added to the bubbles, struggled and tried to dig the claws of his front feet into the slippery floor, but Mr. Dingley was too strong for him. The man lifted him and carried him back to the bathroom, where he dropped him, still struggling, into the tub. This time Ribsy knew he was trapped. He knew he could not scramble out of the slippery tub when he was hemmed in by all these people. He simply stood, dripping and drooping, and waited for whatever was to come next.

Eight small hands and two large hands began to try to rinse him, but they soon discovered that bubble bath was not easy to rinse away. The more they rubbed, the more Ribsy foamed.

"I'm sorry, old boy," said Mr. Dingley. "This is no way to treat a nice dog like you."

At the sound of the sympathetic voice, Ribsy turned a sad face to Mr. Dingley.

"We didn't mean to be unkind," said the man. He took a plastic cup and began to pour water over Ribsy. That seemed to work better than trying to rub the bubble bath off, so the girls ran and got cups and doused Ribsy thoroughly. Still he was not free of bubbles.

"I know. The shower." Mr. Dingley pulled the plug in the tub, drew the shower curtain, reached inside, and turned on the shower.

Ribsy was startled to find water falling down

on him inside a house. This had often happened
out of doors, but never before in a house. It
frightened him. Whimpering, he tried to get out,
first at one end of the curtain and then the other
and then in the middle, where his claws slashed
the plastic.

"Daddy! Don't let him out!" screamed Zibby.

Mr. Dingley finally had to duck under the
shower curtain and hold Ribsy. "That's all right,
boy," he soothed, as his shirt became soaked.
"We'll have you fixed in no time." Ribsy was re-
assured, and stopped struggling.

"With that much bubble bath he didn't leave a
ring around the tub, and so we don't have to
scrub it," observed Zibby, when the ordeal was
over and her father had gone off to change into
dry clothes.

"That's nice." Mrs. Dingley sounded tired.

Ribsy shook himself as hard as he could, spray-
ing the girls and the bathroom with drops that
still smelled of violets. He was soon surrounded
by towels and rubbing hands. He did not mind

being dried—Henry Huggins had always dried
him after a bath—but he did object to smelling
like violets. He felt that if he could manage to
get free of those hands, to get out of the bathroom, he could run away from the smell.

"He's still pretty damp," said Mrs. Dingley,
when they grew tired of rubbing Ribsy. Now that
the family had a wet dog on its hands no one
knew quite what to do with him. "I wish we had
left him on the parking lot where we found him."

"I always knew it would be fun to have a dog,"
said Louanne wistfully.

"We'd better not let him catch cold," said
Zibby. "We might not get a reward for him."

"I'll turn up the furnace," said Mr. Dingley, ap-
pearing in a dry shirt. "Maybe we can coax him
to stand over the heat."

But Ribsy, persuaded to the furnace outlet, did
not care to stand over it. He did not like breathing
hot, dry, violet-scented air. He pulled away from
Zibby, who was trying to hold him. Seeing no
way to escape from the house, he jumped up on

a comfortable chair, as was his habit in the Huggins' house when no one was looking, and tried to curl up into the smallest possible space.

Mrs. Dingley, who was a very calm woman, was not that calm. "Don't let him lie in that good chair when he's all wet," she said, and her husband pulled the unwilling dog to the floor.

"Maybe we could use Mother's hair drier," suggested Zibby. "We could dry one piece of him at a time, starting with his head."

"He would never stand still for that," answered her father.

"My, it's warm in here," said Mrs. Dingley. "There must be some way to dry a dog without roasting the whole family."

Ribsy tried to jump on the couch and was pulled to the floor.

"I know!" Mrs. Dingley had an inspiration. "I once read in that pet column in the paper that one way to dry a dog is to take him for a ride in a car with the heater turned on. It seemed like a silly idea at the time, but it might work." It also might get all the children and the dog out of the house for a while, so she could enjoy a little peace and quiet. She was beginning to feel she needed it.

The girls all agreed that this sounded like fun. "Can we, Daddy? Please, can we?" they begged.

Mr. Dingley was amused. "I guess it wouldn't hurt to give it a try," he conceded. "And I can dry my hair at the same time. Get your jackets on."

Mrs. Dingley reached for a mop to start swabbing out the bathroom.

And so Ribsy, along with four girls and George, was bundled into the station wagon; the windows were closed and the heater turned on. Mr. Dingley drove aimlessly around the neighborhood while the girls petted and consoled the damp dog. As Ribsy began to dry, the windows of the station wagon began to steam. Mr. Dingley wiped the windshield with the back of his hand so that he could see to drive, and the girls polished their windows with their sleeves. Ribsy tried to curl up on the seat and ignore the whole situation as best he could, but Zibby boosted him to his feet. "You won't dry all over if you lie down," she explained.

Gradually Ribsy, whose hair was medium-long except on his ears, where it was short, and on his tail, where it was long, dried. He felt more comfortable, and the mean hungry flea no longer bothered him. It had been driven off by the bath, or perhaps it was too stunned by its experiences to bite. In some ways things were better for Ribsy, but in another way they were worse. He still smelled of violets, except that no violets ever smelled that strong. The perfume of violets is sweet and gentle. Ribsy reeked.

Louanne buried her face in his hair. "M-m-m," she inhaled. "You smell pretty. Just like flowers."

"He must be the cleanest dog in the U.S.A.," remarked Zibby.

Ribsy's sensitive nose did not care at all for the pretty smell, which was not only unpleasant to him but made him uneasy. Smelling strongly of violets as he did, he could not smell anything else. A dog depends on his nose to tell him a lot of things, the most important of which is the presence of danger.

"He certainly smells strong," said Mr. Dingley. "Like a whole field of violets." He turned the car toward home, and as he drove he began to sing.

"Sweet vi-o-lets,
Sweeter than all the roses."

The girls were delighted. They had never heard this song before. "Sweet vi-o-lets," they joined in. "Sweeter than all the roses." It was a good song for singing at the top of their voices, and that was the way the four girls and their father sang.

"Sweet vi-o-lets,
Sweeter than all the roses.
Covered all over from head to toes,
Covered all over with sweet vi-o-lets."

When they finished the verse, they started all over again.

Ribsy did not enjoy the singing. It was just noise to him. He flopped down on the seat and tried to ignore the girls, but he could not. He was too warm; he was surrounded by the unwanted smell; and the girls were too noisy for his sensitive ears.

The singers were carried away by the song as they drove into the garage. "Sweet vi-o-lets," they were singing as loud as they could while they tumbled out of the station wagon. "Sweeter than all the roses."

No one remembered to hang onto Ribsy, who knew an opportunity when he saw one. He leaped from the station wagon, slipped past the girls, and burst out of the garage into the damp and the dusk, where he began running as fast as he could run, down the driveway and across the road and across some woodsy vacant lots toward the highway. Behind him the singing stopped.

"He got away!" shrieked Zibby.

"Catch him! Catch him!" screamed the younger girls.

"Hey, come back here!" called Mr. Dingley.

Ribsy paid no attention. His feet were on asphalt now, and he was going fast, putting as much distance as he could between himself and all those girls and George. The voices grew faint in the distance, but Ribsy kept on running.

After a while he felt safe from the girls, but still he ran, trying to outrun the smell of violets. This he could not do, and when at last he could run no more he stopped and rolled in the dirt and gravel in a ditch at the edge of the highway, to try to free himself from the hated smell. He rolled and rubbed and wriggled on his back with his four feet in the air, but nothing helped. The smell clung no matter what he did.

Panting, exhausted and hungry, Ribsy lay in the ditch and wondered what to do next.

3
Ribsy and Mrs. Frawley

"WE'VE gone back to the parking lot twice to look for Ribsy," said Mr. Huggins late in the afternoon on the Saturday Ribsy had disappeared. "We've called the Humane Society three times to see if someone has brought him in. Now the only thing left to do is advertise in the newspaper."

Mrs. Huggins picked up a pencil and paper from the desk. "What shall we say?" she asked.

"Lost: the best dog in the whole world," said Henry, who was looking out the window hoping to see Ribsy finding his own way home.

"Henry," said his mother, "it won't do any good to keep staring out the window."

"In books dogs find their way home," said Henry. "They travel miles and miles, but they always come home."

"But the lost-and-found notices are full of ads for dogs that apparently can't," said Mr. Huggins. "And when I was a boy I knew some people who lost their dog, and six years later they found it living a mile away."

"Ribsy is smarter than that," said Henry. "And he likes it here. The dog you're talking about probably ran away."

"To get back to the ad," said Mrs. Huggins. "How are we going to describe Ribsy?"

"Medium-sized, patchy spots, and a long tail," said Mr. Huggins. "The trouble with Ribsy is that so many dogs look like him."

"Not to me they don't," said Henry.

"Then think of something different about Ribsy," suggested Mrs. Huggins. "Something that would help identify him. Remember, he isn't wearing his collar."

Henry thought the matter over. He did not want to believe his dog was just like any old dog. There had to be something different about him. What was different about Ribsy, aside from his being the friendliest, most companionable dog in the world? Ribsy hung around the school yard, but so did every other dog that had a boy in school. He followed the mailman, but so did lots of other dogs. Sometimes the Klickitat Street mailman had so many dogs following him he would call "Column right," or "Column left," whenever he crossed the street. Ribsy could sit up and beg and he could shake hands, but so could. . . .

"Hey! I've got it!" Henry exclaimed suddenly. "He's left-handed. I mean left-pawed. He always shakes hands with his left paw!"

About that time rain began to fall again on

muddy, violet-smelling Ribsy as he loped down the highway in the dark. Now he was not only bewildered, he was frightened as well. Unused to being out at night except on his own block on Klickitat Street, he found the world a strange and scary place. A gasoline truck, roaring down the highway dragging its dancing chain against the pavement, terrified him. Speeding cars came so close he was forced to run along the rocky edge of the pavement, and his paw pads, accustomed to lawns and sidewalks, began to hurt. And worst of all, the smell of violets clung and confused his sense of smell no matter how often he stopped and rolled.

Even though he was tired and footsore, Ribsy kept on traveling along the highway, because he somehow knew that this was the direction from which he had come. Once another dog startled Ribsy, who had not caught his scent through the violets, and after he and Ribsy had sniffed one another, the stranger made it plain that a perfumed dog was not welcome in *that* neighbor-

hood. Ribsy did not even have the spirit to argue the matter. He slunk away with his tail between his legs. After glancing back over his shoulder at the dog, who was standing there defying him to return, he began to run again.

When Ribsy had run until he could run no more, he knew he had to find a place to rest out of the rain. The first shelter he found was a gasoline station, which had been locked up for the night. There was a roof over the three gasoline pumps. Ribsy curled up against the center pump, which made a shield against the wind. Shivering, he fell asleep in an aura of violets and gasoline.

Early the next morning Ribsy was awakened when the owner of the station came to work. "Beat it, mutt," said the man. He was not angry, but he did not want a dog getting in the way.

Ribsy obeyed. He was cold, damp, stiff, perfumed, and hungry, which was all bad enough. He did not want to be unwelcome, too, so he trotted off down the highway, looking for a way to improve his situation.

He had not gone far when his nose caught a familiar smell that was strong enough to rise above the now-fading violets. Coffee! To Ribsy that smell meant breakfast. Not that Ribsy drank coffee. In the Huggins household coffee was always bubbling in the electric pot when Henry opened the refrigerator door to get out the dog food for Ribsy. Thus the smell of coffee had come to stand for breakfast to Ribsy just as it did to people.

Ribsy let his nose lead him to the source of the coffee smell, a window that was open a few inches at the rear of a small white house, set back from the highway. Ribsy could hear someone moving around in a kitchen. At home when Ribsy was outdoors and wanted to be fed he scratched at the door. That was what he did now. When the door was opened by an old lady, Ribsy lifted his ears and wagged his tail hopefully.

"My goodness!" exclaimed the old lady, whose name was Mrs. Frawley. "A dog. Shoo! Go away!"

Her voice was not unkind, so Ribsy whimpered hopefully and wagged his tail harder. That coffee smell must mean that dog food was near.

"Shoo." Mrs. Frawley started to shut the door in Ribsy's face. She had shooed dogs out of her yard for so many years that it had become a habit with her. Then the eager, beseeching look on Ribsy's face must have caught her attention, because she hesitated.

Ribsy moved a step closer.

"I believe you're hungry," said the old lady.

Ribsy sat down and held up his left paw. This often pleased people.

It pleased Mrs. Frawley. "Why, Mr. Dog, how do you do?" she inquired.

"Wuf!" answered Ribsy, who felt that the situation looked hopeful.

"Did someone dump you out on the highway to get rid of you?" she asked, because this often happened here, at the edge of the city.

"Wuf!" said Ribsy agreeably. He was making every effort to be charming.

Mrs. Frawley relented. "All right. You look like a nice dog. I'll give you something to eat. Don't go away."

Ribsy had no intention of leaving, especially when he heard the refrigerator door open.

Mrs. Frawley relented even further. She returned to the door and pushed it open. "You must be cold. Come on in. This is my day to scrub the kitchen floor, anyway."

Willingly Ribsy entered the kitchen, and the door was shut behind him.

"Now let's see," mused Mrs. Frawley. "What can I find for a dog to eat?" There was not much in her refrigerator. Mrs. Frawley, whose husband was dead and whose children were grown, lived alone. "How would you like a scrambled egg?" She looked at Ribsy's eager face. "Two scrambled eggs?" She poured a bowl of milk and set it on the floor. While Ribsy lapped thirstily she set about scrambling two eggs, which she set on the floor beside the empty milk bowl. Ribsy sniffed and then licked cautiously, and as soon as the eggs had cooled enough he wolfed them down and looked hopefully for more.

"You *are* a hungry dog," said Mrs. Frawley, and agreeably scrambled two more eggs. "And you smell so nice. Like violets." While she watched Ribsy eat she could not help thinking that it was pleasant to prepare breakfast for someone once more, even if it was only a dog.

Mrs. Frawley was a very lonely person. Her eyesight was not as good as it used to be, and she could no longer crochet or read very much.

Mrs. Frawley was a person who liked to keep busy. Her days were long, because she had little to do and no one to talk to—at least not until Ribsy had appeared at her back door.

With four eggs in his stomach, Ribsy felt much better. He was warm, too, and after exploring the kitchen he walked into Mrs. Frawley's small living room. It was a fussy room full of artificial flowers, crocheted doilies, little pictures, and figurines. The carpet was soothing to his sore paw pads and, after looking around, Ribsy curled up in front of the gas heater and went to sleep.

"Just as if you lived here," said Mrs. Frawley, and smiled. She washed her breakfast dishes quickly and wiped up Ribsy's muddy paw prints. Then she put on her best hat, coat, and galoshes, and took her pocketbook and umbrella, and quietly left the house. She started her old car and, still smiling, drove slowly off down the highway, ignoring the cars that honked at her to go faster. Mrs. Frawley's social-security check had arrived the day before. She felt like going on a little spree after church.

Ribsy did not awaken until Mrs. Frawley returned. When he went to the back door to be let out, she said, "Just a minute. I have a surprise for you. Something I found at the supermarket. Aren't we lucky it's open on Sunday?"

She opened a bundle and took out a leash and red collar, which she fastened in place. The collar was trimmed with rhinestones. Mrs. Frawley liked things fancy. Ribsy did not mind. He struggled only a little bit when she dressed him in a nice warm plaid coat. He was used to wearing a

collar, but the coat puzzled him. He shook himself, but it did not come off. He tried standing on three legs and scratching at it with his left hind foot, but that did not work either.

"My, don't you look nice," said Mrs. Frawley, and led Ribsy out the door.

Still puzzled, Ribsy walked along on the end

of the leash. Mrs. Frawley allowed him to pause by bushes, and then kept on walking him along the edge of the highway. He was agreeable to this, because it was the direction in which his instincts told him he should be going.

"Morning, Mrs. Frawley," said a tottery old gentleman, who had shuffled out to get his morning paper from a round metal box fastened to a post. "See you have a dog."

"Yes," she answered. "Someone must have brought him outside the city limits and dumped him. I don't know what makes people do things like that."

The old gentleman shook his head. "I've taken in so many stray cats my daughter says we don't have room for any more. Just last week we gathered up three more and put them in gunnysacks, and she drove them into town to the Humane Society." He looked Ribsy over. "Seems like a nice fellow. I always wondered why you didn't get some kind of an animal, living all alone the way you do. What do you call him?"

"Rags," answered Mrs. Frawley, after a moment's hesitation. "His name is Rags."

"Pleased to make your acquaintance, Rags," said the old gentleman.

"Anything interesting in the paper this morning?" inquired Mrs. Frawley. "I've stopped taking it. Since they raised the price, I decided there was no sense in spending the money when my eyes are getting so bad. I can get the news on the radio."

"Nothing much." The old gentleman glanced at the headlines. "They are talking about raising property taxes again."

But the old gentleman was mistaken. There was something in the paper that would have interested Mrs. Frawley if she had seen it. Toward the back of the second section under "Lost and Found" were three small lines of type that read:

LOST at shopping center: mongrel dog, black, white, brown. Answers to Ribsy. Shakes hands with left paw. No collar. AT. 7-4139. Reward.

"Come on, Rags," said Mrs. Frawley, tugging at the leash. "Time to go home now."

This time Ribsy resisted, because he did not want to go back. He wanted to go on down the highway that led toward Klickitat Street. Mrs. Frawley pulled while Ribsy braced all four feet.

"Nice doggie," coaxed Mrs. Frawley. "Come on home, Rags." She pulled harder at the leash.

Ribsy finally had to give in and, remembering the breakfast Mrs. Frawley had so kindly given him, he did not mind too much. He would get away soon.

Inside the little white house once more, his new mistress removed the leash and blanket and, holding out her hand, said, "Shake hands, Rags."

Ribsy obediently extended his left paw.

Then Mrs. Frawley got busy. She prepared a nice stew with meat and carrots and onions, the first she had cooked in a long time. She served Ribsy a generous helping for lunch. Ribsy was not used to lunch, only breakfast and dinner, but he did not object. After lunch he was taken for another walk on the end of the leash, and then he had a long nap, which he needed after eating so much. For dinner he had another serving of stew and a cupcake. That night he was allowed to sleep on the living-room couch, which Mrs. Frawley had thoughtfully covered with an old blanket. This was a pleasant change from the pile of gunnysacks he slept on in the Huggins' basement. There was no doubt about it; Ribsy, although not particularly happy, was mighty comfortable.

The next day was much the same, and the next and the next, except that one evening after supper Mrs. Frawley asked Ribsy to sit up. "Sit up, Rags," she said.

This, too, was familiar, so Ribsy sat up. Then he hiccuped. He was not used to three large meals and a cupcake for dessert.

"Good dog," said Mrs. Frawley, and smiled as if she suddenly had an idea.

The next day Mrs. Frawley drove off once more in her old car. She returned with a doll's straw hat, a pair of false spectacles, and a corncob pipe. She put the hat on Ribsy's head, balanced the spectacles on his nose, and poked the stem of the pipe into his mouth. "Sit up, Rags," she said.

Ribsy dropped the pipe and sat up.

"No, no," cried Mrs. Frawley. "You're supposed to hold the pipe in your mouth." She put the stem in place again, and Ribsy sat there, not understanding what it was all about, but knowing that Mrs. Frawley was pleased. "Good boy!" exclaimed the old lady happily. She removed the pipe and gave Ribsy a piece of dog candy. "My, won't you be a big surprise!" She spent the evening teaching Ribsy another trick, saying his prayers with his nose on his paws, propped up against the couch. It was not hard to do and it seemed to please the old lady, so Ribsy was agreeable.

For the next few days Mrs. Frawley bustled about cleaning house. She washed windows, polished silver, and vacuumed under the cushions of the couch. Ribsy did not care for the smell of ammonia or the sound of the vacuum cleaner, but whenever he asked to go out Mrs. Frawley always willingly dropped her work and took him out on the leash.

As the days went by Ribsy became restless. Even though his stomach was much too full, he still wanted to get out and run. He wanted to chase a ball and run after a boy on a bicycle. Sometimes, when he heard boys calling to one another, he would go to the window and whimper. Still, he did like the old lady, who fed him three meals a day and let him sleep on the living-room couch. Unfortunately, his stomach was so full he spent more time thinking about running than actually trying to escape so he could run. He would put his paws up on the sill of the living-room window, look out at the grass and the highway, and go take another nap.

Soon after the housecleaning there came a day when Mrs. Frawley was extra busy in the kitchen. She got out her best dishes, which she rarely used anymore, and washed them. Then she baked sev-

eral kinds of cookies and gave Ribsy a sample of
each. Mrs. Frawley was getting ready for a meeting of her club.

Mrs. Frawley's club was made up of fifteen
ladies her own age, who lived alone or with their
children or in old people's homes. They met once
a month, and this month it was Mrs. Frawley's
turn to entertain them. Those who still had cars
and could drive were to pick up the others and
bring them to Mrs. Frawley's little white house at
two o'clock in the afternoon, because they did not
like to drive after dark.

At a quarter to two Mrs. Frawley did an un-
usual thing. She took Ribsy into her bedroom,
and said, "Now be quiet, Rags. Not a peep out
of you." Then she went out and shut the door.

Ribsy was so stuffed it was a great effort for
him to jump up on the bed. He curled up and
dozed off, and as he dozed he was aware of car
doors slamming and ladies laughing and talking.

Out in the living room the ladies, each one
carrying a parcel, were busy greeting one an-

other and talking about their grandchildren. Each
lady thought her grandchildren were smarter
than any other lady's grandchildren, and each
lady became just a little impatient with the others
for talking about their grandchildren when she
wanted to talk about her own grandchildren.

Finally Mrs. Frawley put a stop to all the brag-
ging about grandchildren by clapping her hands
and saying, "I think we should begin. Who wants
to be first?"

For this meeting each lady brought something interesting to show the other members of
the club. It was like Show and Tell in school,
only the old ladies did not call it Show and Tell.
One lady brought a Civil War sword that had
belonged to her grandfather. Another brought a
beautiful shell, another a primer she had used in
the first grade over seventy years ago. One lady
brought a clay turtle her grandson had made.
The other ladies secretly thought this was not
very interesting and that their grandchildren
could do much better.

Mrs. Frawley saw to it that her turn came last. "You ladies will have to excuse me a minute," she said, and went into the bedroom and closed the door. "Wake up, Rags," she whispered, and when Ribsy drowsily opened one eye she put his little straw hat on his head and slipped the elastic under his chin. Next she balanced his spectacles on his nose. "Come on," she whispered.

Ribsy jumped heavily to the floor and trotted after Mrs. Frawley, who poked the stem of the corncob pipe between his teeth just before she led him into the living room.

"Ladies!" cried Mrs. Frawley, as if she was a master of ceremonies. "Presenting Rags, the newest member of the family!"

The ladies of the club all gasped and applauded. Ribsy was so confused by all the people staring at him that he dropped his pipe.

Mrs. Frawley picked it up and poked it into his mouth once more. "Sit up, Rags," she directed. "Sit up, boy."

Obediently Ribsy sat up. All the ladies

laughed. "Isn't that cute?" they murmured. "Isn't that adorable? Just like a little old man."

"Good boy," approved Mrs. Frawley. "Now say your prayers, Rags." Ribsy, who had not minded performing his tricks when he was alone with Mrs. Frawley, did not want to say his prayers in front of all these strangers. He did not like to be stared at and laughed at. He felt embarrassed and ashamed. He tucked his tail between his legs and tried to slink back to the bedroom.

The ladies all laughed. "He's bashful," someone said.

"No, no, Rags," said Mrs. Frawley, seizing him by the collar and pulling him to the couch. "Say your prayers."

With great reluctance, Ribsy sat up with his paws against the couch and rested his nose on them. The ladies were delighted. They laughed and clapped their hands. Ribsy gave Mrs. Frawley a mournful now-can-I-go look and slunk behind the couch, where he brushed off the hat and spectacles with his paws. Then he flopped down on the carpet and felt very, very unhappy. His sharp ears caught the sound of a boy calling, "Hey, Jack!" someplace outdoors, and he felt even more unhappy. Ribsy was a dog and not a person. He wanted to be treated like a dog once more, even if it meant sleeping on gunnysacks in the basement. He wanted to eat dog food and horsemeat, and roll on the grass, and chase balls, and run after boys and bicycles. This afternoon had been too much for him. Ribsy was determined to escape.

Mrs. Frawley explained to her club what she thought was true—that her dog was one of the many unwanted animals that were dumped along the highway, that other dogs had come to her door and she had shooed them away, but that this one was such a smart, friendly dog, who could shake hands, that she felt she just had to take him in. Then she served her guests ice cream and cookies and set a saucer of dessert on the kitchen floor for Ribsy.

Ordinarily Ribsy would have trotted into the

kitchen to investigate when he heard the thump
of a saucer being set on the floor, but not today.
He was not going to come out from behind that
couch and be laughed at by all those old ladies.
Besides, he was not hungry. He dozed and
waited.

Soon after the ice cream and cookies had been
eaten the meeting broke up. The ladies with cars
were anxious to start home before the evening
traffic. The way people drove these days, they
said, it was a wonder there weren't more acci-
dents than there were. Several guests peeked over
the couch and said, "By-by, doggie." They were
wishing their children or the old people's homes
they lived in would let them keep pets.

Ribsy paid no attention, but when he heard the
door open, he edged forward and peered around
the couch. The ladies were all busy buttoning
their coats, wrapping their interesting objects,
picking up their canes, and saying good-by to one
another. No one was paying any attention to the
dog behind the couch. Ribsy waited for a clear

path to the door, and when he saw it, he bolted so fast his feet slipped on the edge of the floor where there was no carpet. He fell, picked himself up, leaped down the steps, and shot across the yard to the highway as fast as he could go. It felt good to stretch his legs and run once more. Ribsy's tongue flapped and his eyes shone. He was a dog again!

Behind him he heard Mrs. Frawley calling, "Rags! Rags! Come back here!" She was too late. Ribsy was on his way toward dog food and balls to catch and bicycles to chase. Mrs. Frawley would have to find another dog to keep her company, and in her neighborhood that should not be hard to do.

4
Ribsy Becomes a Mascot

THE Hugginses had received a number of telephone calls in answer to their advertisement. A man had seen a dog that sounded like Ribsy running down Broadway, but he did not know where the dog had gone. A lady had been feeding a stray spotted dog for over a month, and she would really like to get rid of him. A boy called to say he knew a couple of dogs that sounded like Ribsy, and how much was the reward? Another lady called to say she didn't know anything about Ribsy, but she did have five perfectly adorable puppies and she would be glad to give Henry one.

It was late in the evening, after the advertisement had been running for several days, that **Mr. Dingley**, the father of the four girls and George, telephoned to say that he had read the notice and that he was sure it must have been Ribsy his family had picked up in the parking area at the shopping center. He told the tale of finding Ribsy, of the bubble bath, and of Ribsy's disappearance into the dusk. He was sorry he had not called sooner, but three of his children had come down with chicken pox and he had been busy.

"Bubble bath!" Henry was disgusted when his father had relayed the story to him. "A bunch of dumb girls giving Ribsy a bubble bath, for Pete's sake! No wonder he ran away."

"At least we know the direction in which Ribsy went," said his mother. "That's something."

"We'll let the ad run awhile longer and see if it won't bring results," said Mr. Huggins.

"Bubble bath," muttered Henry. "Bubble bath!"

By the time the advertisement had run for

three weeks, the Hugginses had received several more calls and gone to look at three different dogs. None of them was Ribsy.

"Well, Henry, I don't like to say this," said Mr. Huggins at last, "but I think we might as well stop the ad."

Henry nodded. He could not think of anything to say. He was sure Ribsy had to be someplace, that someone must have him, but that someone quite plainly was not going to answer an advertisement in a newspaper. And why should he? Ribsy was such a good dog, anyone would want to keep him.

By now Ribsy was back inside the city limits. He had learned from his own neighborhood on Klickitat Street that many people fed their pets outside the back door or in the garage. This made his search for food fairly easy as he continued his journey. He had only to investigate backyards, and sooner or later his nose led him to a dish with a few crumbs of food or, if he was lucky, to a whole bowlful. Unfortunately, most of the people whose yards he passed through kept cats. He gulped down several meals of rather fishy cat food.

Workmen, eating lunches out of lunch buckets, were another source of food. Workmen, tearing up the streets; workmen, repairing telephone wires; workmen, putting new roofs on old houses —all of them were glad to share a corner of a

sandwich or a bite of a doughnut with a friendly dog.

Hunger was not Ribsy's problem. He was no longer sure of the way toward home. None of the streets he followed seemed to lead to Klicki-tat Street. He searched for something familiar, something that would lead him home to Henry Huggins. He trotted along the sidewalk, looking up at all the people he met, hoping that one of them would turn out to be a member of his family. They were always strangers, but Ribsy was not easily discouraged. He continued his search until he came to a mailman waiting for a bus. Ribsy, who had often followed the Klickitat Street mail-man on his rounds, was delighted to see someone who looked a little bit familiar. He pranced right over to the bus stop and wagged his tail.

"Hello, Pooch," said the mailman.

Encouraged, Ribsy sat down beside the mail-man, who obligingly patted him. That, as far as Ribsy was concerned, was that. He would follow the mailman, who was sure to lead him to the

Huggins' house. When the bus stopped and the mailman swung aboard and sat down, Ribsy scrambled after him and flopped down at his feet.

"Hey," said the driver. "That dog can't ride on this bus."

"He's not my dog," said the mailman.

"Somebody get him out of here fast," said the driver. "I got a schedule to make."

A high-school boy was glad to help. He seized Ribsy by the collar and pulled. Ribsy stiffened his legs and dug his toenails into the floor of the bus. He was not going to go. The boy pulled so hard at his collar he began to choke.

"Don't you hurt that poor dog," cried an old lady from the back of the bus. "Take your hands off him this instant, or I shall report you to the S.P.C.A." The boy let go of the collar.

"Wait. I have an idea," said the mailman. He slipped the strap of his mail pouch off his shoulder, got up, and walked quickly down the aisle.

Ribsy was not going to be left behind. He

trotted right down the aisle and followed the mailman out the rear door of the bus. The mailman then surprised him by sprinting to the front door and jumping into the bus once more. Before Ribsy could jump in after him, the door was shut in his face and the bus drove off in a particularly smelly cloud of exhaust.

Ribsy had never had a mailman treat him this way before. He did not know what to think. At first he tried running after the bus, but the smell of its exhaust soon discouraged him.

He wandered along the sidewalk until he saw three girls carrying brown paper bags. Instantly Ribsy's spirits rose. Here was a familiar sight. Girls with lunches in paper bags were sure to lead him to school, and there he would find Henry. He followed happily along behind the girls, just close enough to catch a whiff of their lunches. Tuna fish, peanut butter, and pot roast. That pot-roast sandwich smelled delicious.

"Don't look now, but there is a dog following us," said one of the girls, and giggled. The other two thought this was very funny. They all giggled and glanced back at Ribsy, who trotted along minding his own business.

Sure enough, just as Ribsy expected, the three girls led him to a familiar place, a two-story red-brick school, surrounded by a fenced-in asphalt playground. His spirits rose even higher. Henry must be around somewhere. After noticing that the three girls left their lunches on a bench before they went off to play hopscotch, Ribsy put his nose to the ground and ran around the school yard, searching for the scent of Henry Huggins. He picked up many scents of boys in sneakers, but none of them had the exact scent of Henry.

Ribsy also picked up the scent of the pot-roast sandwich once more, and this time he helped himself to the lunch bag. There was no use letting a perfectly good piece of meat go to waste when he had eaten so much fishy cat food lately.

"Look!" squealed the owner of the pot-roast sandwich. "That dog has my lunch!"

The chase was on. Everyone, boys and girls,

big and little, chased Ribsy. He loved it. He hadn't had so much fun since he had been lost. He ducked and dodged with the brown paper bag in his mouth. Sometimes, when he was far enough ahead, he dropped the bag a second and stood panting, with a laughing look on his face, as if to say, Catch me if you can. Then, when someone almost reached him, he snatched up the lunch and ducked and dodged some more.

Finally the yard teacher blew a whistle that hurt Ribsy's ears, and everyone stopped chasing him.

"Here, doggie," coaxed the yard teacher. "Nice doggie."

Ribsy eyed the teacher warily, ready to run if she should decide to chase him.

Instead she approached him slowly with her hand extended. "Nice doggie," she said. "Give us the lunch. That's the boy." She was so friendly Ribsy let her pet him and take the lunch.

"The poor dog is hungry," said the owner of the undamaged pot-roast sandwich.

"I'll give him something out of my lunch," someone said, and a dozen lunch bags were opened.

"Now children, you know dogs are not allowed on the school grounds." The yard teacher spoke in a mild voice because, after all, Ribsy was such a nice friendly dog.

No one seemed to hear her. Ribsy found himself being offered pieces of sandwiches, potato chips, carrot sticks, raisins, and cookies. He accepted the most appetizing bits, to the delight of the givers, while those who bought their lunches in the cafeteria petted him and wished they had something to feed him. Ribsy could tell he was going to like this place.

When the bell rang, Ribsy went right into the school with the boys and girls and into the nearest classroom, which happened to belong to Mrs. Sonchek's second grade. He looked around the room at the desks and blackboards and at an empty aquarium on a ledge below the window. None of this was especially interesting to him.

Then he walked into one door of the cloakroom at the back, sniffed the lunches and wraps, and walked out the other door. Satisfied with his investigation, he flopped down near the cloakroom door and laid his nose on his paws. He had spent the night dozing in a cold garage, and was glad of a chance to nap in a warm, dry place that smelled pleasantly of sneakers, lunch bags, and boys and girls.

The thirty boys and girls of Mrs. Sonchek's second grade took their seats, while Ribsy dozed off. Suddenly he was awakened by the sound of thirty pairs of feet sliding out from under their desks and thirty boys and girls standing up.

Everyone was going someplace, and Ribsy was about to be left behind. He jumped to his feet, too.

"I pledge allegiance," began the class, "to the flag of the United States. . . ." They were not going anywhere, after all.

After the flag salute the class sat down—all but the two boys nearest Ribsy, who petted him in such a way that Ribsy knew he had somehow pleased them.

A girl raised her hand.

"Yes, Penny?" said the teacher.

"Mrs. Sonchek, there is a dog back here, and when we stood up for the Pledge Allegiance, he stood up, too!" Penny was pleased to have announced this news to the class.

Everyone turned in his seat to admire such a smart animal.

"It must be a very patriotic dog," said Mrs. Sonchek pleasantly. "And now, Danny, will you please take him outdoors?"

Reluctantly, with several backward glances, Ribsy allowed Danny Yaxley to lead him outdoors, where the asphalt was cold and unfriendly after the warm floor of the schoolroom. Ribsy looked sadly at the door that closed behind him, and the minute the milkman came to deliver the boxes of milk cartons, he slipped inside, returned to the second-grade room, and flopped down by the cloakroom door.

Penny waved her hand. "Mrs. Sonchek, that dog is back."

"Keep quiet!" whispered the boys.

Mrs. Sonchek merely said, "The dog is not bothering anyone, Penny. Pay no attention to him." Mrs. Sonchek did not like to waste classroom time. There were so many interesting and important things to learn in the second grade.

That was how Ribsy became a member of the second grade. He spent his nights in garages whose owners had left the doors open. In the morning he went to school with the neighborhood children, who fed him bits of their lunches and, in a day or two, began to bring him an occasional dog biscuit. When he was thirsty, he had only to go to the drinking fountain in the school yard and some boy always turned it on for him. After he had managed to lap the spurting water with his tongue, the boy usually had a drink, too.

Following the flag salute, when he was sure of being petted if he stood up, he dozed all morning, going out at recess with the rest of the class.

At lunchtime he got in line and went to the cafeteria, where he finished the sandwiches of those
who asked him to—except peanut-butter sandwiches. These Ribsy would sniff and politely re-
fuse. Peanut butter stuck to his teeth. After lunch
he lay at the back of the room with his nose on
his paws, waiting for school to be out so that he
could play with anyone who wanted to play with
a friendly dog. It was a pleasant life.

This had gone on for several days. Then one
day at lunchtime Ribsy lined up as usual and went
to the cafeteria. He was very well-behaved,
stayed with his class, and sat down beside a table
where Mrs. Sonchek's bag lunchers were eating

while the rest of the class lined up to buy their lunches. He was licking the remains of a crunched-up potato chip from the floor when he became aware of a man standing over him.

"And who is our friend?" asked Mr. Woody, the principal.

"A dog," said Bill Amato.

"A nice dog," said Penny Moyce.

Ribsy was pleased when the principal stooped to pet him. "Whose dog is he?" asked Mr. Woody.

"Search me," said Pete Schlictman. "He comes to school every day. He lives around here someplace. See, he has a collar." He pointed to the red collar Mrs. Frawley had bought for Ribsy.

"I know," said Mr. Woody. "I have seen him. Perhaps he belongs to someone who is away at work all day. From the fancy red collar, I would guess he belongs to a lady."

"Oh, please let him stay," begged Penny. "He's an awfully good dog. He even stands up for the Pledge Allegiance." Mrs. Sonchek's bag lunchers nodded.

Ribsy wanted to please this man, so he held up

his left paw. Mr. Woody smiled and shook hands. "Well, fellow, I see you are a southpaw."

Ribsy, always glad of attention, stood up and wagged his tail.

"It looks as if Mrs. Sonchek's room has a mascot," said Mr. Woody. "As long as he behaves himself."

Mrs. Sonchek's bag lunchers beamed at the principal. "Our mascot is always good," said Penny earnestly, and the others nodded.

The week went smoothly until Friday arrived. Friday in Mrs. Sonchek's room was Show and Tell day. It started like any other day. Mrs. Sonchek looked around the class, and noted that Danny Yaxley was absent. Ribsy stood up with the rest of the class for the flag salute and then flopped down for a nap.

"Does anyone have anything to share with the class this morning?" asked Mrs. Sonchek.

Kathleen Adelson came to the front of the room to show off her doll, which had a pair of real little sunglasses. The boys looked scornful.

Pete Schlictman showed a tool chest he got for

his birthday. He said his mother would not let him use the hammer or saw in the house. The boys looked interested. They wished they had tool chests, too.

Philip Gorberg had just finished telling about the time he was riding down a hill with his father and the brakes of the car refused to work, when the door of the classroom opened. Danny Yaxley came in with his mother, who was carrying a sheet of corrugated cardboard and a wooden box with holes bored in the sides. It was a rule in Mrs. Sonchek's room that anyone who brought a pet for Show and Tell had to bring his mother, too. The mother's job was to take the pet home.

"I'm sorry we're late, Mrs. Sonchek," said Mrs. Yaxley, who looked as if she had not taken time to put on her lipstick. "Danny insisted on bringing his squirrel for Show and Tell. The cage was too big to carry, and I had to stop and bore holes in this box and, well—I am not very good at boring holes."

All the boys thought this was funny. They were sure they would be good at boring holes. The

class was excited. They were going to get to see a
real live squirrel right there in school.

"My squirrel is gnawing on the box!" Danny's
eyes were bright with excitement.

"A live squirrel!" exclaimed Mrs. Sonchek, smiling bravely. "But how can we see it in a wooden
box?"

"Danny said the aquarium was empty, and we
could put Frisky in it with this cardboard over
the top." Mrs. Yaxley looked apologetic. The
whole thing was not her idea.

"Yes," said Danny enthusiastically. "Frisky will
look real nice in the aquarium." The class was
delighted. A squirrel in an aquarium!

"All right, Danny." Mrs. Sonchek gave her
permission.

"I'm sorry to take up so much classroom time,"
apologized Danny's mother, as she put the
wooden box down inside the aquarium. "Now
Danny, hold the cardboard over the top and clap
it down quickly when I take my hands out." She
slid back the lid of the box.

Ribsy, who had opened one eye when he heard

the murmurs of excitement from the children, caught a whiff of squirrel. He did not even stop to think. He automatically jumped to his feet, barking.

"Oh!" Startled, Mrs. Yaxley gave a little scream and jumped away from the aquarium. She had not noticed Ribsy.

Danny dropped the cardboard. A gray squirrel with a bushy tail darted out of the box and sprang up on the edge of the aquarium.

Ribsy put his paws up on the counter and barked furiously. That squirrel did not belong in here.

"Ch-ch-ch-ch," chattered Frisky, and ran along the counter below the windows with Ribsy following on the floor. The class laughed and shouted.

"Catch him!" cried Mrs. Yaxley.

A boy grabbed Ribsy by the collar. Ribsy pawed the air with his front feet and strained at his collar until he choked.

Mrs. Sonchek pounded on her desk with a ruler. "Class!" she cried. "Class, please!"

How could any class be quiet with a squirrel loose in the room? Nothing that interesting had happened since Billy Amato had brought a live clam to school. Frisky jumped to the top of a pile of supplementary readers in the front of the room and, from there, he took a flying leap to the staff that supported the flag in a bracket above the blackboard.

Ribsy broke loose and ran under the flag. He put his paws in the chalk tray and made as much noise as he could. He would show that squirrel who belonged in this room. Frisky ran lightly up to the end of the staff that held the flag and scolded Ribsy. This infuriated Ribsy and delighted the class. If this kept up, there would be no time at all for arithmetic.

"People!" cried Mrs. Sonchek, banging on the desk with a ruler. "People, please!"

Then the door opened, and Mr. Woody, the principal, entered followed by Mrs. Hildebrand, the school nurse. At the sight of the principal the class became a little quieter. Not much but a little.

"I'm terribly sorry," said Mrs. Yaxley, wringing her hands. "I didn't mean to take up so much classroom time."

Mr. Woody frowned at the class. "Quiet!" he ordered. "What's going on in here?"

This time the class obeyed, but Ribsy did not. Neither did Frisky, who flirted his tail and scolded. Mr. Woody grasped the situation.

"Someone hold the dog," said the principal. Three boys ran to the front of the room. One tackled Ribsy, and the other two grabbed his collar.

"Mrs. Sonchek, get me a jacket," directed the principal.

"Here, take mine." Danny pulled off his jacket and handed it to Mr. Woody.

Ribsy, straining at his collar, panted hoarsely. These boys were spoiling his fun.

"Quiet, everyone," repeated the principal. He walked to the front of the room and stepped up on one of the chairs in the reading circle. "Now Mrs. Sonchek, when I lift the flag down, you throw the jacket over the squirrel."

Ribsy made strangling noises while the class, quiet at last, waited breathlessly to see if the principal's plan would work. This was much better than a live clam.

Slowly the principal reached for the flagstaff, and slowly he lifted it from its bracket above the blackboard. The squirrel stopped chattering. Slowly, slowly the principal lowered the staff. Never had Ribsy wanted to leap at anything as much as he wanted to leap at that squirrel. Slowly, slowly Mrs. Sonchek lifted Danny's jacket. "Ch-ch-ch," scolded Frisky. Ribsy, who would accept anything from people, even a bubble bath and a little straw hat and spectacles, resented the sassiness of that squirrel. He growled.

Frisky leaped from the flagstaff. Mrs. Sonchek tried to throw the jacket over him, but it fell empty to the floor while Frisky ran lightly along the chalk tray, hopped to the floor, and ran under the teacher's desk. Mrs. Sonchek picked up the jacket and prepared to try again, while Mrs. Yaxley and Mrs. Hildebrand took jackets from the cloakroom and prepared to stalk the angry squirrel.

Mr. Woody replaced the flagstaff in its bracket, and armed himself for the chase with the yardstick Mrs. Sonchek kept on the chalk tray to use as a pointer. When some of the boys started for the cloakroom to get their jackets too, Mr. Woody said sternly, "In your seats, class." There were enough people running around already.

Mr. Woody rattled the ruler under Mrs. Sonchek's desk. Frisky darted out and ran down an aisle. The three women threw jackets and missed, while Ribsy barked and strained at his collar. The girls pulled their feet up from the floor. The boys sat on their desks to get a better view.

"Mr. Woody," said one of the boys who was holding Ribsy, "why don't we let our mascot chase him? I bet he could catch him."

"No!" said one half of the class, mostly girls, who felt sorry for the squirrel.

"Yes!" said the other half, mostly boys, who wanted to see a dog catch a squirrel.

"Don't you dare sic that dog on my squirrel,"

said Danny to the boy who was holding Ribsy's collar.

"Class!" cried Mrs. Sonchek.

The squirrel skittered into one of the cloakroom doors. Naturally the whole class had to turn around to face the back of the room. Ribsy could hardly stand it. If they would just let him go, he could show that squirrel a thing or two.

"Now we've got him," said Mr. Woody. "Line up with the jackets at the other door, and I'll go in with the yardstick and chase him out."

The three women stood at one door of the cloakroom with the jackets aimed, while Mr. Woody marched in the other door with the yardstick. Thumping and whacking could be heard from the cloakroom. "Look out! Here he comes!" yelled the principal. The teacher, the mother, and the school nurse crouched with the jackets. There was a flash of gray fur, and all three pounced.

"I've got him!" cried Mrs. Hildebrand, the school nurse, who was on her knees clutching a wiggling jacket.

"Quick! Roll him up," said Mrs. Yaxley. She took the rolled-up squirrel and stuffed it, jacket and all, into the wooden box.

Ribsy felt the boys' hold on his collar relax. He made pathetic coughing sounds.

"Hey, that's my jacket," said Billy Amato.

"I'll bring it back before lunch period," promised Mrs. Yaxley.

"My mother isn't going to like it if that squirrel chews up my jacket," said Billy.

Mrs. Yaxley looked as if she had had a difficult morning. "If he does, I'll buy you a new one," she said in desperation. Turning to the principal, she added apologetically, "I'm terribly sorry to have taken up so much classroom time."

"But won't the squirrel smother?" asked Penny Moyce.

"He's not rolled up that tight," answered Danny's mother, who was in a hurry to get the squirrel home to his cage.

"I never did get to tell about my squirrel," complained Danny.

"Never mind, Danny. You showed him, and that is enough." His mother spoke sharply before she escaped from the classroom with Frisky safe inside the box.

It was all over. The class slid back into their seats and waited to see what Mr. Woody would say about the interesting time they had had when they were supposed to be learning arithmetic.

The principal came to the front of the room and gave Ribsy a stern look. Then he faced the expectant class. "Boys and girls." Mr. Woody sounded very serious. "Dogs are not allowed on the school grounds." The class looked guilty. They all knew this, but it was Mr. Woody himself who had called the dog their mascot.

"And I'm afraid I made a mistake in making an exception—" Mr. Woody looked once more at Ribsy.

Now Ribsy looked guilty. He understood he had done something wrong, but he was not sure what it was. He thought dogs were supposed to chase squirrels and get rid of them.

"—but this dog looked like such a friendly dog," continued Mr. Woody, "and he seemed so well-behaved that I overlooked the rule."

Ribsy waved his tail wistfully to show that he did not mean to do anything wrong, that he was really a very nice dog.

"Now we know," said Mr. Woody, "that a dog does not make a good mascot and that the rule is right. This should be a lesson for all of us. I'm afraid the dog will have to go."

"Oh—" The class made a sad sound. They loved their mascot and did not want him to go. Neither did they want this morning, which had been such fun, turned into a lesson in obeying rules.

When Mr. Woody looked at Ribsy, the dog stopped waving his tail and let it droop. He knew he had not succeeded in making everything all right again. He hung his head and looked dejected.

"Come on, boy," said Mr. Woody kindly, and took hold of Ribsy's collar. "Come along with me."

One of the girls in the front row began to cry. The whole class waved, and those in the last row of seats patted Ribsy as Mr. Woody led him out of the room. Mr. Woody did not let go of Ribsy's collar outside the classroom or even outside the building. He kept a tight grip until he had led Ribsy outside the metal fence that surrounded the school yard. Only then did he let go of Ribsy. He slammed the gate with a clang, and said, "Good-by, fellow."

Ribsy understood one thing. He was no longer wanted. This made him unhappy, and when Ribsy was unhappy he seemed to droop all over. He took a few steps away from the gate, stopped, and looked hopefully back. Maybe the man would change his mind and call him so that he could come running.

The man had not changed his mind. "Go home," he said firmly and kindly.

Go home. That was a command that Ribsy understood. He had heard it many times on Klickitat Street when he had run through the neighbors' flower beds. He had heard it when Henry did not want him to chase after the car. Now the words reminded him of Henry Huggins and the familiar street with green lawns and trees.

"Go home," repeated the principal.

After one more sad backward glance Ribsy started walking. He wanted to obey the man. He wanted to go home, but he did not know where home was, and there was no way he could make the man understand.

5

Ribsy Goes to a
Football Game

"HENRY, I have an idea," said Mr. Huggins at
breakfast one morning, about a week after he
had discontinued the advertisement for Ribsy in
the newspaper. "This afternoon I'll get off from
work early, and we'll go down to the Humane
Society and pick out another dog."

"I don't want another dog," said Henry. "I want Ribsy or nothing."

"Henry, be reasonable," said his mother. "Ribsy has been gone almost a month. If we were going to find him, we would have found him by now."

"I am being reasonable," said Henry. "I just want my dog, is all. He's got to be someplace. He'll come home as soon as he can make it. I know he will. Maybe somebody has him tied up, and he's chewing on the rope right now. How would he feel when he made it home and found some other dog eating out of his dish?"

"I don't know about that, Henry," said his father. "Ribsy is no Lassie. He's just an ordinary city mutt."

"Maybe somebody has him fenced in, and he's trying to dig his way out," said Henry, ignoring his father's critical remark. "I bet that's what he's doing right this minute. Digging under a fence."

But Ribsy was not digging under a fence. Neither was he gnawing through a rope. He was

trotting along the sidewalk enjoying the fall sun-
shine. His ears were up, his eyes were bright, and
his tail was waving. Ribsy was getting used to
being lost. He was beginning to enjoy it. He met
so many nice people—not so nice as Henry Huggins, but nice just the same. Except for sleeping
in drafty garages and occasionally being forced
to make a meal of fishy cat food, Ribsy found a
lot to enjoy in the life he was leading.

As Ribsy trotted along the sidewalk, he became
aware of lines of cars, bumper to bumper, filling
the street. Each car was jammed with yelling,
shouting high-school students, some of them waving pompons of crepe paper fastened to sticks.
This was a stimulating sight to Ribsy, who felt
that with so many noisy young people around
something interesting was bound to happen.

"Zachary Taylor High School! Rah! Rah! Rah!"
shouted one carload of students. "T-T-T-A-Y.
Y-Y-L-O-R. T-A-Y. L-O-R. T-a-a-ay-lor!"

"Down with Taylor," shouted another carload.
"Hooray for Chester A. Arthur High!"

Ribsy did not understand what it all meant, but it sounded like fun. He trotted faster, and soon he saw a mob of high-school students crowding toward some narrow openings in an enormous gray concrete wall. Naturally Ribsy had to investigate to see what all the excitement was about, and so he, too, joined the crowd. He wove his way through a forest of legs until he came to one of the gates, where a man was taking tickets.

"Beat it, mutt," said the man in a most unfriendly way.

Ribsy was not discouraged. He was a cheerful dog, who knew there were many friendly people in the world. He wriggled his way through more legs until he came to another gate where another man was taking tickets.

"No dogs allowed." This man gave Ribsy a shove with his foot.

From inside the wall came the sound of many voices yelling. Something was going on that Ribsy should not miss. He tried a third gate.

"Get lost, Pooch," said the third ticket taker.

Ribsy was still not discouraged. He simply sat down to wait for some change in the situation that would allow him to enter this strange place. The wait was not unpleasant, because many people stooped to pet him while they stood in line with their tickets to await their turns at the gate. Among the crowd were several boys about Henry Huggins' age, but none of them was Henry.

Gradually the crowd began to thin. A delicious smell floated across Ribsy's nose. He sniffed hungrily and swallowed. Hot dogs! There were hot dogs someplace inside this strange wall. Ribsy moved closer to the gate, wagged his tail, and fixed the gatekeeper with his most eager, pleading look as memories of home and hot dogs passed through his thoughts. Henry Huggins was fond of wienies and often ate one after school. Of course, he always gave one to his dog.

"Scram," said the gatekeeper, reaching for the ticket of a straggler.

Ribsy sat down and held up his left paw. This had worked before. It might work again.

"I see you're a southpaw," remarked the gate-keeper, who was more sociable now that he had no tickets to take. "Well, offering to shake hands won't do you any good. You still can't come inside this stadium."

Ribsy whimpered.

"No southpaw pooches allowed," said the man. "Now beat it."

Ribsy had no intention of leaving. Some ancestor of his had waited patiently at a rathole. He would wait patiently at this gate. He lay down with his nose on his paws and waited. It was not easy to be patient. The sounds from inside told him he was missing something exciting, and those hot dogs smelled so good he could hardly stand it. This was one of the days he had been forced to eat cat food. He lay watching and waiting and thinking about hot dogs for what seemed like a long, long time.

Inside, a band began to play, and voices began to sing. Ribsy did not enjoy this as much as shouting, but even though music bothered his sensitive ears, he could appreciate the enthusiasm of the people. There was more yelling, and then a scream went up from the whole crowd, and a man's voice boomed out over a loudspeaker.

Ribsy did not care at all for the loudspeaker, which hurt his ears, but did not hurt them enough to drive him away. Hunger, curiosity, and the desire to be in on the excitement held him to his vigil at the gate.

A boy about Henry's age, wearing jeans patched on both knees and on the seat, appeared at the gate. "Hey mister, can I go in?" he asked. "The game has started and the stadium isn't full."

The man hesitated before he answered, "Sure, kid. Go on in."

After that the gatekeeper kept his eye on Ribsy, and Ribsy kept his eye on the gatekeeper. Inside there was more screaming. Someone pounded a drum and someone rattled a cowbell. Ribsy closed his eyes. He would fool that man. He looked as if he was asleep, but he was not. He was letting his nose and ears tell him the man was still there guarding his gate.

"T-T-T-A-Y," shouted the students from Zachary Taylor High School. "Y-Y-L-O-R. T-A-Y. L-O-R. T-a-a-ay-lor!"

The man moved a few feet from the gate. He was so busy trying to see what was going on inside that he did not notice Ribsy flick one eye. After a few minutes he glanced back at the dog, who was apparently sound asleep. Satisfied that the dog would not try to get into the stadium, the man moved farther inside and up the ramp that led to the grandstand seats. Ribsy's eyes opened a hair's breadth and closed again. The man took a chance and moved even farther from his post.

After making sure the gatekeeper had his back turned, Ribsy sprang to his feet, dashed through the gate, and around the concrete wall that surrounded the field. Even if he had been wearing jingling license tags, he could not have been heard above the uproar inside. When he was a safe distance from the gatekeeper he trotted up a ramp, where he could see what was going on inside this strange and interesting place.

What Ribsy saw inside that stadium was enough to excite any red-blooded dog. The sun was shining down on thousands of lively boys and girls, all of them jumping up and down and yelling, and many of them eating hot dogs. Below him lay an enormous field of grass, nice flat grass, just right for running on. There wasn't a rock or bur or thistle on the whole field. And on the grass there were boys, quite a few boys, in football gear, running and tumbling all over one another. There were also three men in striped shirts, who appeared to be running after the boys. And that was not all. The boys had a football for chasing! A dog really could not ask for much more.

Ribsy was delirious with the joy and excitement of it all. He longed to get down there on that grass to romp with the boys and chase that ball. He barked wildly.

"Hey, look! A dog," said a boy, sitting on a bleacher near Ribsy.

"Maybe we better get him out of here," said a second boy, who was eating a hot dog.

"Aw, he can't hurt anything way up here," said the first boy, his eyes on the football game below.

Ribsy looked at the hot dog and swallowed. The boy obligingly broke off a piece and dropped it on the concrete for Ribsy, who gobbled it up. It was the first food he had had in a long time that tasted like home. He wished he had more.

For some strange reason the two boys were now pounding one another on the back. "Boy, oh, boy!" one of them was saying. "A touchdown for Taylor High!" Then he stuffed the last of his hot dog into his mouth.

Ribsy lost interest in the boy after that, and wandered up and down the steps that separated the rows of bleachers. He had never seen so many obliging people in one place before in all his life. All he had to do was sit down and stare at someone eating a hot dog, and a piece was almost sure to be broken off and dropped at his feet. At first Ribsy gobbled up both the bun and the wienie, but in a little while he became choosy, rejecting the bun if it had mustard on it and finally skipping the bun altogether and just swallowing the wienies.

With familiar food in his stomach and so many kind people around him, Ribsy was happy. He began to look for a way to get in on the excitement below. He trotted along the wall that rimmed the field, and when the cheering was especially loud he put his paws up on the edge of the wall and barked. He was barking from sheer excitement and also because he saw below him some boys about Henry's age, who were standing on the edge of the field trying to look important.

"Look!" squealed a girl. "A dog cheering for Taylor High!"

"Isn't he darling?" said another girl. "Look at his cute collar trimmed with rhinestones. Maybe we should make him our mascot."

A boy said, "Somebody better get him out of here. A dog can wreck a football game," but the game was so exciting, with the score seven to six in favor of Zachary Taylor High, that no one wanted to take his eyes from the players long enough to remove a dog from the stadium. One team grabbed the ball and raced toward one end of the field. Before the boy who carried the ball was able to cross the line for a touchdown, the other team managed to capture the ball and went racing off to the opposite end of the field. The game was so close that no one was paying any attention to Ribsy. He was free to explore the stadium. One team made a touchdown, and then the other team made a touchdown. Finally, down at the end under the scoreboard, Ribsy found a ramp that led through a sort of tunnel that opened on that nice green grass.

"We want a touchdown! We want a touchdown!" the crowd was chanting.

Since all the boys Ribsy had ever known who tumbled around on grass were glad to have a dog romp with them, Ribsy ran out on the field confident that he was welcome. The grass was so cool to his paws and so fragrant to his nose that he had to stop for a good roll. With his four feet in the air he squirmed and wriggled. It was bliss. Only the fun of chasing a ball made him stop.

The quarterback from Chester A. Arthur High School had the ball, and was running down the field toward the end zone with the Zachary Taylor team after him. The boys and girls in the grandstand were a screaming, yelling mob. The hands on the clock on the scoreboard showed that only seconds were left to play, and those seconds were passing quickly.

Naturally Ribsy wanted to chase after the fastest runner, the boy who was carrying the ball. He raced down the edge of the field, avoiding the younger boys, who, to his delight, had begun to chase him. A newspaper photographer, anxious to photograph the moment that would decide the game, ran along the side of the field with the boys chasing Ribsy. To Ribsy this was all part of the fun.

"Come on, Arthur!" screamed half the mob, who attended Chester A. Arthur High School.

"Tackle him! Tackle him!" screamed the other half, who attended the Zachary Taylor High School.

This was the most fun Ribsy had enjoyed since the boys and girls had chased him around the school yard with a lunch bag in his mouth. He eluded the younger boys, who were chasing him along the side of the field. When he was opposite the quarterback, who was carrying the ball, he put on a burst of speed and darted onto the field in front of the player. Ribsy hoped he would drop the ball, so he could have a turn chasing it.

The Arthur High School quarterback was so busy trying to stay ahead of a player who was about to dive at his knees that he did not see the dog. Just before he would have crossed the line for a touchdown, he tripped over Ribsy, fell flat on his face, and dropped the ball, which was snatched up by a player from the Taylor High School team. Flashbulbs popped. The last second ticked off the clock on the scoreboard. The referee blew his whistle. The crowd went wild. Drums boomed. Cowbells rattled. The game was over. Thanks to Ribsy, Zachary Taylor High School had won, thirteen to twelve.

To Ribsy's surprise, he found himself tackled, not by a football player, but by a boy about Henry's age. The knees of his jeans were patched, and his hair had not been cut for some time.

"Gotcha!" said the boy, hanging on tight. It was all a game to Ribsy.

"That your dog?" asked a photographer.

The boy saw a chance to be important for a few minutes. "Sure," he said. "Sure he's my dog."

Ribsy stopped struggling, because he needed

to pant. He let his tongue hang out of his mouth while he tried to catch his breath.

"What's his name?" inquired the photographer, pulling out a pencil and paper.

"Junior," answered the boy promptly. It was the first name that popped into his head, and the reason it popped into his head was that Junior was his own nickname. It was a nickname he did not like one bit.

"Junior." The man wrote it down. "That's a funny name for a dog."

"He was named after his father," the boy answered quickly.

"What's your name?" asked the photographer.

"Joe Saylor," answered the boy, leaving off the Junior on purpose.

"Address?"

Joe told where he lived, a street half a mile from the stadium.

By now the Zachary Taylor High School students were swarming around Joe Saylor to pet the dog that had helped to win the game. Under the circumstances, Joe was not going to put Ribsy down, not when everyone thought it was his dog who was the hero of the game. It began to seem to Joe that Ribsy really was his dog. As for Ribsy, he was enjoying the attention he was getting and, after all, Joe was a boy. Ribsy liked boys.

Joe carried Ribsy off the field. Every time he was about to put Ribsy down, someone said, "That's the dog that saved the game." Boys were satisfied to pet Ribsy, but girls were inclined to squeal and say, "Isn't he darling?" Some of them hugged him, and one girl went so far as to kiss him.

Both Joe and Ribsy were having a good time. It was not until the crowd had thinned out that Joe released Ribsy. Joe then went up into the grandstand. Not having anything better to do, Ribsy tagged along. Joe walked along between the rows of seats, looking for something, and Ribsy walked along, too. Joe picked up a nickel and a penny, and several rows farther up the stadium he found a dime, someone's hot-dog change that had been dropped and had rolled away during the excitement of the game. Ribsy examined wads of waxed paper that had been wrapped around hot dogs. It was getting dark before Joe found another nickel, and by that time the stadium was almost empty.

"Only twenty-one cents," Joe remarked to Ribsy. "I do better at college games." When Joe left the stadium, Ribsy followed. It seemed almost like old times, when he used to follow Henry.

"Where are you going?" Joe asked Ribsy. Then he bent to examine the dog's collar under a streetlight. There was no license tag. Joe shrugged and started toward home. One of his shoes was untied, and his shoelace flopped as he walked. Ribsy did not have anyplace to go, so he went along, too.

When Joe came to an old house with a sagging porch and peeling paint, Ribsy followed him around to the back and right up the steps. Inside someone was practicing on a piano. *Plink, plunk, plunk,* over and over.

Joe groaned. "Mom's making Darlene practice," he muttered.

Ribsy looked expectantly at the door, which he was sure would be opened for him. A boy like Joe would not leave a dog out on the porch now that it was suppertime.

"Don't you have anyplace to go?" Joe asked Ribsy.

Ribsy's answer to this was a short, eager bark. It turned out that Ribsy was right about Joe. The boy bent over and took off the red rhinestone-trimmed collar that old Mrs. Frawley had given Ribsy. He stuffed it into his pocket, and said, "That's a sissy collar for a dog like you." Then he opened the door, and said, "Come on in."

Ribsy stepped onto the worn linoleum of the kitchen floor, and Joe closed the door behind him.

DOG WINS GAME

DOG NAMED JUNIOR: Dog...
football game at city stadium
coach commented that...

RIDED A
WOLF DVI...
CAVICE...
No...

6

The Famous Dog

HENRY HUGGINS was zigzagging down Klickitat Street on his bicycle delivering *Journals*. Out of habit he glanced back over his shoulder to see what Ribsy was doing. Of course, Ribsy was not there. It had been a month since he had loped after Henry's bicycle, and still Henry could not get over the feeling that Ribsy was following him. A dull, heavy sensation filled Henry, as it always did when he forgot and looked back for Ribsy.

Henry flung a *Journal* extra hard. A month.

Ribsy could have chewed through a dozen ropes and dug under a dozen fences. The girls who gave him the bubble bath did not live more than ten miles away. A healthy dog like Ribsy did not need a month to walk ten miles, even if he did have to stop and chew through a rope or two and tunnel his way under a few fences. Even allowing for a dog fight now and then, it should not take Ribsy a month to walk ten miles.

"Hi, Henry!" It was Henry's friend Beezus, walking down the street with her little sister Ramona. Ramona was busy stepping on all the cracks just to show she wasn't afraid of breaking her mother's back. "Has Ribsy come home yet?" asked Beezus.

"Nope." Henry paused by the curb, even though he did not feel like talking about Ribsy, not even with Beezus, who, for a girl, was very sensible.

"Ribsy was such a nice dog," said Beezus.

Ramona stopped stepping on cracks. "Why don't you get a horse instead?" she asked.

"Oh, Ramona, don't be silly," said Beezus. "Henry couldn't keep a horse in the city."

"I'd look pretty funny delivering papers with a horse following me," said Henry.

"You could ride him," Ramona pointed out.

Henry felt a little ridiculous. Of course he would ride a horse if he had a horse. He would gallop down Klickitat Street flinging papers from his saddlebags. He would be something like Paul Revere— "Aw . . ." muttered Henry, wondering how Ramona had managed to get him off on such a wild train of thought. "I don't want a horse."

"I do." Ramona went on stepping on cracks.

Henry pedaled slowly, leaning to the right and then to the left, as if pushing bicycle pedals was hard work. Ribsy was not coming back. He knew it now. He might as well stop telephoning the Humane Society and leaving food in the dish on the back porch. He might as well throw away the old tennis ball.

Maybe Ribsy had found a home he liked better.

Maybe he had found a home with some rich boy, who fed him T-bone steaks instead of canned dog food and horsemeat. Maybe the rich boy's mother let him sleep on the foot of the rich boy's bed. Maybe the rich boy's family let him ride in their new car all the time without making him chase through the rain first.

While the piano in the Saylors' living room went *plink, plunk, plunk*, Ribsy sat down in front of the refrigerator in the Saylors' kitchen. Joe, who was turning out to be the kind of boy Ribsy expected him to be, obligingly opened the refrigerator door and, after looking around, helped himself to a handful of raw hamburger, which he held out to Ribsy.

Mrs. Saylor's voice came from the living room. "Is that you, Junior?"

"Yeah," answered Joe above the *plink, plunk, plunk* of the piano. Only then did he remember to slam the refrigerator door.

"What are you doing in the refrigerator?" asked

his mother, as the piano stopped plinking and plunking.

"I'm not in the refrigerator. I'm in the kitchen." Joe laughed at his own joke, and did not bother to mention that he was feeding a stray dog, who was gobbling the raw meat out of his hand.

"None of your back talk. Where have you been all this time? Go on, Darlene, go on with your practicing. I was worried sick about you," said Mrs. Saylor.

"I went to the high-school football game like I told you," answered Joe, as Ribsy finished the last of the hamburger and licked his hand to make sure he hadn't missed any. "I asked if I could go, and all you said was we didn't have any money for football games. I didn't need any money, so I went."

"How did you get in?" asked Mrs. Saylor. "Go on, Darlene."

"Same way I always do," answered Joe, wiping his hand on the seat of his pants and going into the living room. Ribsy stayed behind to lick his

chops. "I hung around until one of the gatekeep-
ers let me go in. Nobody cared. The stadium is
never full for high-school games."

"Joe Saylor, Junior!" exclaimed his mother.
"Just look at you! Now tie your shoe and tuck your
shirttail in and go wash your face. And Darlene,
go on with 'The Pussycat Waltz.' I am not paying
out perfectly good money for your piano lessons
and then not have you practice." Mrs. Saylor was
inclined to be snappish when she was trying to
get Darlene to practice.

Ribsy was curious about these people in the
living room, so he followed Joe to investigate. A
girl a couple of years younger than Joe was sitting
on a round piano stool. She was a thin, wiry girl,
who appeared to be all knees, elbows, and ponytail. Her hair was full of plastic—a plastic ban-
deau, plastic barrettes, and a plastic clasp around
her ponytail. Mrs. Saylor was standing beside her
pointing to the music on the piano and saying,
"Here I scrimp and pinch to give you piano lessons—" Then she saw Ribsy. "Joe Saylor, Junior!

What is that dog doing in my house?" she demanded.

Ribsy knew from the way she pointed at him that she was talking about him. He distrusted the tone of her voice, and his tail drooped.

"I dunno." Joe shrugged his shoulders. "He just followed me." He was watching his sister twirl around on the piano stool with her ponytail flying. If she twirled in the same direction long enough, the top of the stool would come unscrewed and she would fall over. Darlene, however, had it nicely timed. Just as the stool was about to topple she began to twirl in the opposite direction.

"Well, he can just follow you right out," snapped his mother, who was finding her son exasperating.

Joe heaved a gusty sigh. "Oh, all right. Come on, dog."

Obediently Ribsy followed Joe to the back door and allowed himself to be let out. "Don't mind her," whispered Joe, whose shirttail was still hanging out. "She just talks that way when she's trying to make old Darlene practice."

The hamburger in Ribsy's stomach was filling but cold. Not having anything better to do, he sat down on the back porch. He liked Joe and he liked hamburger, so he decided he might as well stay for another meal. If he sat by the door long enough, the boy was sure to come out again.

Plink, plunk, plunk went the piano once more. As the chill left the hamburger in his stomach, Ribsy curled up beside the washing machine and dozed off until the woman's angry voice inside the kitchen woke him.

"Joe Saylor, Junior!" she was saying. "Do you mean to say you fed perfectly good hamburger to a *dog*? Why, that was our supper. Now what are we going to have?"

The piano playing stopped. "Mama, can we have pizza pie?" Darlene asked eagerly. "I'll go to the store."

"It's after dark and, besides, I don't have money for pizza pie," answered her mother crossly. "Just wait till your father hears about this."

Ribsy did not care for the sound of an angry voice, so he got up, shook himself, and took a stroll around the neighborhood. He barked at a smug-looking cat sitting on a porch. When it did not budge he went on his way. It was no fun to try to chase a cat that would not run. He exchanged sniffs and tail wags with a couple of dogs, who did not seem to mind his being there, and after he had satisfied himself that the neighborhood was reasonably friendly, he trotted back to the Saylors' house and curled up by the washing machine again. The smell of macaroni and cheese that came from the kitchen did not tempt him, because his stomach was full of hamburger, so he went to sleep.

In the morning, when he heard people stirring in the kitchen and smelled coffee, Ribsy sat hopefully by the back door waiting for someone to open it. He even whimpered a few times, but there was so much noise inside, with people arguing, the radio playing, and Darlene dawdling over the practicing she had not finished the day before, that no one heard him.

Mrs. Saylor had not forgotten about the hamburger. "And he fed perfectly good hamburger to a stray dog!" She could not get over it. "Sometimes I wonder what goes on in that boy's head."

"Kids like dogs," said a man's voice. "Maybe we should get him one."

Plink, plunk, plunk. Plink, plunk, plunk.

"Now if that isn't just like a man," said Mrs.

Saylor. "I have enough trouble buying groceries for four people and paying for Darlene's piano lessons and making payments on the TV without taking on a dog."

"It is now thirty-four minutes past seven," said the radio.

"Look," said the man. "I've got trouble of my own. One of my best customers brings a dress in to be cleaned, and now I can't find the belt. If I don't find that belt by the time she comes in to get her dress this afternoon, I'm going to lose her business, and we can't afford that. The dog is gone and we didn't starve, so forget it."

"It is now thirty-five minutes past seven," said the radio.

But the dog was not gone, as Joe discovered when, sometime later, he barged out the back door with his lunch bag in hand. He was going so fast he fell over Ribsy and dropped his lunch, which Ribsy began to sniff. His nose detected the fragrance of bologna.

Joe picked himself up and rescued his lunch.

"You still hanging around?" he asked, as he started off to school.

Ribsy followed close to Joe with his nose against the lunch bag.

Joe understood. He opened the bag and took out half a bologna sandwich, which he handed to Ribsy, who wolfed it down before he caught up with Joe. He enjoyed following a boy to school again, and pranced along with his ears and tail erect. When they reached the school, Joe pointed to a sign on the metal fence around the school yard. "See. It says no dogs allowed." He stooped to pet Ribsy before he went through the gate.

Ribsy sat down for an enjoyable twenty minutes of watching what went on inside. Girls jumped rope or played kickball. Boys tossed a ball back and forth or chased one another. Girls squealed, boys yelled, Ribsy barked. It was a very pleasant interval, until the buzzing of a bell put an end to it all and the boys and girls disappeared into the building.

Ribsy then explored the neighborhood by daylight, took a nap by the school-yard fence, and spent recess and lunch period watching the boys and girls. Several times Joe spoke to him through the fence. The day seemed familiar to Ribsy, because he had followed its same pattern with Henry Huggins so many times. After school he followed Joe home just as he had followed Henry many times. It all seemed so natural that Ribsy was beginning to forget Henry and to feel that he belonged to Joe.

Joe seemed pleased to have Ribsy at his heels.

Before he opened the back door he whispered, "Come on in, and let's see what happens."

Ribsy followed Joe into the kitchen, where Mrs. Saylor was ironing.

"Junior, tuck your shirttail—is that dog *still* here?" she demanded.

This time Joe tucked his shirttail in. "I guess he likes it here."

"Don't you think he belongs to someone?" asked Mrs. Saylor.

"He sure didn't act like it when he started following me around in the stadium," said Joe.

Ribsy wagged his tail. Mrs. Saylor had not

sounded as cross as she had the day before, when she was worn out trying to get Darlene to practice.

"How do you expect to feed a dog?" Mrs. Saylor wanted to know.

"He's only a medium-sized dog," Joe pointed out. "And I found twenty-one cents in the stadium after the football game."

"Twenty-one cents. How far do you think twenty-one cents will go these days?" his mother asked.

"It ought to buy one can of dog food."

Mrs. Saylor shook her head and sighed, but she did not order Ribsy out of the house.

"Are we going to get to keep him?" asked Darlene, when she came home from school a few minutes later and found Ribsy in the kitchen.

"Ask your father," answered her mother. "Now wash your hands and practice your piano lesson."

That evening Ribsy was served a supper of beets, cold leftover macaroni and cheese, and a crust of bread and margarine that Darlene had refused to eat, even if eating crusts was supposed to make her hair curly. Ribsy, who was not a choosy dog, had eaten meals that he had enjoyed more. After supper he slipped into the living room and curled up on the carpet. He might as well assume he was welcome until someone told him he was not.

Mr. Saylor settled back in his favorite chair, the one with the sagging springs, to read the evening paper while Mrs. Saylor occupied herself pasting her Blue Chip stamps in a little book. Mr. Saylor was in a good humor, because he had found the belt of his customer's dress that day. Joe sat down on the floor in front of the television set to watch a detective program. Darlene chose that moment to practice "The Pussycat Waltz."

"Dad, make her stop," said Joe. "She hasn't practiced all day, and the minute I want to look at TV she has to start banging."

"I'm not banging," said Darlene, and added, "Your old program bothers me when I'm practicing." *Plink, plunk, plunk.* She made a great show of sitting up straight and holding her wrists up properly while she played.

"You're just trying to be a pest," Joe informed her, "and to get out of doing your homework."

Plink, plunk, plunk. "Dad, Juney's bothering me when I'm trying to practice." Darlene knew it especially annoyed her brother to be called Juney.

"Cut it out, you kids." Mr. Saylor was paying very little attention to his childen. He was used to bickering.

"Pest," hissed Joe. Gunfire rattled from the television set.

"You're the pest," said Darlene, without missing a beat. "Won't let me practice in peace."

"Ha," said her brother. Darlene didn't fool him one minute.

Ribsy did not care for the piano playing, but he did not mind the bickering. He had heard the boys and girls in his neighborhood talk in the same tone of voice many times.

Suddenly Mr. Saylor looked up from his paper.

"Well, what do you know!" he said. "That mutt you picked up has his picture in the paper. Right here in the sports section."

"Hey, let me see." Joe leaped to his feet and peered over his father's shoulder. There was his dog, photographed at the moment he tripped the football player. It was all in the picture—the running dog, the falling player, the rolling ball.

By now Mr. Saylor was reading the story under the picture. "It says the dog belongs to Joe Saylor, and gives our address. Did you tell them that, Junior?"

"Sort of, I guess," admitted Joe.

Mr. Saylor read on. "It beats me the way newspapers can get things mixed up. It says here the dog's name is Junior." He laughed. "A dog named Junior. That's a good one."

"Yeah." Joe laughed too, less heartily. He felt embarrassed to be found out, but at the same time he was pleased. He could cut out the picture and take it to school to show everyone how important his dog was. That is, he could if his mother let him keep the dog. This was a question he was carefully avoiding. The longer the dog was allowed to hang around, the better his chances of keeping him. So far things looked hopeful.

Mrs. Saylor finished fitting a row of Blue Chip stamps onto a page of the little book before she came to look over her husband's shoulder along with Darlene. "Oh, that dog," was all she said.

Joe stooped to pet the dog he was now sure belonged to him. It said so right there in the newspaper. That ought to convince his family. Ribsy looked up gratefully and thumped his tail on the floor.

Then the telephone rang. "I'll get it," shrieked Darlene, who always liked to get to the telephone first. "It's for you, Dad," she said, disappointed.

"Who is it?" her father asked.

"I don't know. Some boy asked for Joe Saylor."

Mr. Saylor sank back in his chair. "You get it, Junior. It's probably some kid from school."

"Oh, that's right," said Darlene. "Some people do call Juney Joe. I forgot."

Joe tried to trip his sister on the way to the hall to answer the telephone. "Hello?" he said.

"Hello," answered a strange boy's voice. "Uh. . . . Joe Saylor?"

"Yes."

"Well . . . uh, my name is Henry Huggins," said the boy. "Your dog. . . . I mean, how long have you had him?"

"Awhile," said Joe cautiously. "Why?"

"He's my dog," said Henry. "I lost him at the shopping center about a month ago."

"Who is it, Junior?" asked Mrs. Saylor.

"A boy," Joe told his mother, and the answer seemed to satisfy her. "The shopping center," repeated Joe into the telephone, hoping to gain time to think. "That's way on the other side of town."

"I know," admitted Henry, "but my dog got into the wrong car by mistake, and some people took him home, and by the time they saw my advertisement in the paper he had run off, because they gave him a bubble bath, and then they couldn't find him."

Joe had no way of knowing whether what Henry was saying was true or not. It sounded peculiar, that part about giving a dog a bubble bath. He certainly did not want to believe what he was hearing, not when it was beginning to look as if he might get to keep the dog. "Lots of dogs look like my dog," he said. "I don't think he's your dog at all."

"Yes, he is," insisted Henry. "I know he is. I could tell by the picture in the paper."

"Prove it," challenged Joe.

"He always shakes hands with his left paw," said Henry.

Mr. Saylor did not like to listen to people talk on the telephone. "What does the boy want?" he asked, interrupting the conversation.

"Some kid thinks my dog is his," answered Joe. "Says the dog shakes hands with his left paw."

Mr. Saylor laughed. "Tell him you haven't been introduced," he said, and returned to his paper.

"The dog and I haven't been introduced," said Joe to Henry. "We never shook hands."

"But perhaps the dog does belong to the boy," protested Mrs. Saylor.

"Let Junior handle it," said Mr. Saylor.

There was a silence from Henry's end of the line. Joe had a feeling Henry wanted to say something like, Oh, a wise guy. Joe looked down the hall at Ribsy, lying on the carpet, and said, "O.K., if he's your dog, why doesn't he have a license tag?"

"He does have," said Henry, "but when he got lost he wasn't wearing his collar. I took it off, so he could scratch his neck."

Joe felt triumphant. He was still carrying a red, rhinestone-studded collar in his pocket. "But this dog was wearing a collar when I found him." He realized too late that he had given away two bits of information. The dog had no license tag, and Joe had found him.

"He's been gone about a month," said Henry. "Somebody else must have put a collar on him."

"You still haven't proved he is your dog," said Joe. Even though he had given out more information than he intended, he felt he had an advantage in the conversation. He could always hang up if he wanted to.

"My dad says he'll drive me over to your house," said Henry. "You'll see. Ribsy will know me."

"Ribsy," said Joe. "That's a dumb name for a dog."

At the sound of his name Ribsy picked up his ears. He had not heard the word Ribsy for weeks.

"When I first got him he was so thin his ribs showed," explained Henry. "So I called him Ribsy."

"They don't show now," said Joe. "It can't be the same dog. Well, so long."

"Wait!" The boy on the other end of the line sounded desperate. "My dad said he'd bring me over tonight. We're offering a reward for Ribsy."

"How much?" Joe felt it could not be much. Ribsy was no fancy poodle or German shepherd. He was just a mutt.

"Ten dollars."

Ten dollars! Ten whole dollars. Ten dollars was a lot of money to Joe, but he was not going to admit it to Henry, who, he decided, must have lots of money if he could offer a ten-dollar reward for a dog when he could get another just as good free at the Humane Society. Mutts like Ribsy didn't cost anything.

Joe's silence must have worried Henry, because he raised the reward. "Ten dollars and my new flashlight. Can we come over now?"

Joe saw that he was gaining a new kind of advantage. After all, he could get another dog just as good as this one free of charge himself. If he stalled long enough, there was no telling what this boy might offer him. "I don't know," he said, not committing himself. "We're pretty busy. Anyway, I don't think he is your dog. He's happy here."

"I *know* he's my dog." Henry sounded worried. Then he seemed to have an idea. "Hey, I know. Let me talk to him."

This took Joe by surprise. "On the phone?"

"Sure," said Henry, sounding as if he talked to dogs on the telephone all the time.

Joe was scornful of this suggestion. He did not believe a dog would pay any attention to a voice on a telephone, so he did not mind letting the boy try. "Just a minute," he said.

Ribsy heard Joe's fingers snapping for him to come. Obediently he got up and trotted into the hall.

"Here, somebody wants to talk to you," said Joe, holding the telephone to Ribsy's ear.

"Hiya, Ribsy!" Henry's voice came clearly through the telephone so that Joe could hear, too. "How's Ribsy?"

It worked. Ribsy began to bark.

"Ribsy!" Henry was shouting. "Ribsy! It *is* you!"

Well, what do you know? thought Joe. A dog would talk on a telephone.

Ribsy barked harder. He could not understand where Henry could be, but he recognized the voice coming out of the black thing Joe was holding to his ear. Maybe if he barked hard enough, Henry would come out from wherever he was hiding.

"Ribs!" Henry shouted again. "Ribsy!"

Joe, who was now sure of a reward, felt that a conversation that consisted of barks and a dog's name yelled into a telephone was not getting anyplace. Ribsy's nose told him that Henry was not in the living room or even in the house and so, as Joe put the telephone back against his own ear, he ran to the front door. When it was not opened instantly, he began to bark wildly and scratch at the wood. Henry had to be someplace on the other side.

The startled Saylors stared at him until Darlene darted across the room and opened the door.

Still barking, Ribsy ran out into the night. "Ribsy!" The boy's voice came faintly from the telephone in the hall. "Ribsy, what happened to you?"

Back on the Saylors' porch Ribsy heard Joe shouting to his sister, "What did you let him go for? There's a reward for him! Ten whole dollars!"

And Darlene answered, "When a dog wants

out, you're supposed to let him go. How was I to know he was worth so much?"

Then Joe's feet came pounding down the sidewalk behind Ribsy. "Ribsy!" he called. "Ribsy! Come back here!"

Ribsy wasn't going back. Henry was somewhere close by, and he was going to find him.

7

Ribsy and the Apartment House

HENRY pressed the telephone against his ear as hard as he could. He heard a lot of barking, and then he heard Joe yell, "What did you let him go for? There's a reward for him! Ten whole dollars!" There was an answer in a girl's voice, which Henry could not catch, the sound of thumping feet, and then nothing but the sound of a television set, tuned to a program with a lot of shooting, which his parents would not let him watch.

"I don't get it," said Henry to his mother and father, who had been following his side of the conversation. "There was a lot of barking, and now there isn't anyone on the line. Anybody home?" he asked into the telephone in a loud voice. There was no answer, only gunfire from the television set.

"Hang on a minute and see what happens," said Mr. Huggins. "Now that we're this close to Ribsy we can't let him get away."

Henry strained to catch any sound that might come through the telephone. He heard barks that grew fainter, yelling, arguing and finally a click as someone in the Saylor household replaced the telephone receiver. That click was as final as a period at the end of a sentence. Slowly he replaced the receiver. He thought a moment, and then said, "At least Ribsy recognized me. That's something."

When Ribsy could run no more, he flopped down on the sidewalk in the dark to pant. As soon as he had caught his breath he got up again and started off at a brisk trot with his nose to the ground. The trouble was he did not know where he was going. It was all very puzzling. He had heard Henry Huggins' voice, but he could not find Henry. He stopped and barked, thinking that Henry would call. When there was no answer he continued his search, hoping his nose would guide him.

The sidewalk gave Ribsy the scent of many people and of a variety of dogs and of a cat or two, but it did not give him the scent of Henry. Ribsy became tired, confused, and bewildered. Late that night he gave up looking for Henry and went to sleep on the cold concrete in front of the Coffee Cup Café, where the lingering smell of hamburgers, fried during the day, gave him some comfort.

Early the next morning Ribsy woke up, feeling stiff and hungry. The Coffee Cup Café was not open, so he walked around to the back door, where he found a garbage can that smelled interesting. It must have smelled interesting to some other dog, too, because the can had been tipped over and garbage was strewn around the ground. Ribsy helped himself to some bits of bun, which were smeared with more relish than he cared for. He also ate the remains of a piece of pie. The best garbage had already been eaten, but at least his stomach was no longer completely empty.

Ribsy wandered aimlessly around the neighborhood, which did not look at all like Klickitat Street with its green lawns and white houses surrounded by shrubbery. There was very little grass in this neighborhood and not many bushes, although there were a number of fire hydrants. Many of the buildings came right to the sidewalk, and most of them were of brick and were three or four stories high.

It was in front of one of these buildings that Ribsy first saw the boy with the tennis ball. He was a thin boy, somewhat round-shouldered, who was sitting on the front steps tossing the ball from one hand to the other. Naturally Ribsy was interested in a boy with a tennis ball.

While Ribsy was watching the boy, a young woman came out of the apartment house. She was wearing a black coat over the starched dress and apron of a waitress. "Now see here, Larry Biggerstaff," she said, "you keep out of trouble today, you hear?"

"Yeah, Mom." Larry stopped tossing the ball.

Ribsy decided he did not like the smell of this woman. It reminded him of violet bubble bath.

"I don't want to hear any more complaints from the manager about you," continued his mother. "Last Saturday Mrs. Kreech complained that you played a mouth organ in the hall, bounced a ball so that it disturbed the lady downstairs, and tried to climb down the fire escape. Keep it up, and you'll get us evicted, and then where will we go?"

Larry heaved a big sigh to show that he was disgusted with the whole situation. "But Mom, there's nothing to *do*. I don't even have a good ball to take to the playground."

"I don't have money to buy balls," said his mother. "At noon you come to the café and get your lunch. And in the meantime, keep out of trouble." She left the apartment house and hurried down the street toward the Coffee Cup Café.

Larry began to bounce the tennis ball, which was old and had lost much of its life. He had to throw it down hard to make it bounce at all. Nevertheless, the sight was a stimulating one to Ribsy. He pranced right up to Larry and wagged his tail to show that he was ready to play.

Larry did not understand. "Go away, you old dog," he said crossly, and muttered, "I don't even have a good ball."

This boy needed educating. Ribsy barked to tell him that here was a dog ready to play with a tennis ball. Larry backed away.

Ribsy wagged his tail and looked eager, but this only made Larry cautious. Plainly Ribsy would have to show this boy how to play. He bowed before Larry, ran off a little way, and then came dashing back. Larry dropped the ball, and Ribsy picked it up.

"You gimme back my ball," said Larry.

Ribsy dropped the ball and stood over it, wagging his tail.

Cautiously Larry advanced toward the ball, but when he was about to pick it up, Ribsy grabbed it in his jaws and went racing up the street.

"Hey!" yelled Larry.

Ribsy raced back, dropped the ball at Larry's feet, and stood waving his tail and looking hopefully up at the boy.

"Well thanks, pal," said Larry, surprised and pleased.

"Wuf!" answered Ribsy.

The boy finally understood. He threw the ball down the street, and Ribsy bounded after it, darting between the people who were walking along the sidewalk, and catching it on the first bounce. He was delighted and so was Larry. The boy threw the ball again and again for Ribsy to retrieve. Finally Larry sat down on the front steps of the apartment house, and Ribsy threw himself down at his feet to pant.

"You're a pretty nice dog," remarked Larry. "I'd sure like to keep you, but Old Lady Kreech would never let me."

Ribsy laid his nose on his paws and looked up at Larry, who returned Ribsy's gaze. "You hungry?" Larry asked.

Ribsy thumped his tail on the sidewalk. He liked having a boy talk to him.

Larry liked having a dog to talk to. "If you was a big cross dog, I bet Old Lady Kreech would stop yelling at me. She'd be scared to yell if I had a big dog following me around."

Ribsy rolled over on his back and allowed Larry to rub his stomach for him.

"You wait here," said Larry. "No, that wouldn't work. You might run off while I was getting you something to eat. Can you be real quiet?"

Again Ribsy thumped his tail.

"Come on then. I'll get you some cornflakes or a wienie or something," said Larry, and pulled a key out of his pocket. Ribsy followed him up the stairs, and Larry unlocked the front door. Inside he tiptoed past the door of the apartment occupied by the manager of the building to an old-fashioned elevator. Ribsy was ready to enjoy this new game the boy was playing. Larry opened a glass door and folded back a metal gate, and Ribsy followed him into what appeared to be a small square room without windows. Larry closed the gate and the door, and pushed a button on the wall.

There was a whirring noise, and suddenly Ribsy had a feeling he had never felt before. He felt as if he was going up while his stomach stayed down. He did not like the feeling one bit. He did not like this strange little room. He wanted out right now. He began to bark.

"Sh-h-h!" Larry seemed upset about something, because he scowled and grabbed at Ribsy. "Sh-h-h! She'll hear you."

The manager had already heard. A door on the first floor flew open, and a woman's cross voice called up, "Larry Biggerstaff. You get that dog out of this building at once!" It was the kind of voice that could make a dog slink away feeling guilty.

By that time the little room had stopped at the second floor. Larry slid back the gate and opened the glass door. Before he stepped out, he whispered, "You stay right here. I'll come back and get you in a minute." Then he left the frightened dog and shut him in the little room. Ribsy did not know what to do. He did not want to stay in the little room alone, but there was no way he could get out. He was even afraid to bark, so he made little anxious noises. Suddenly he felt himself beginning to rise again while his stomach seemed to stay behind. He barked for Larry to come and get him out of this place, but all he heard was the whir of machinery and the thump of Larry's sneakers running downstairs.

As the elevator stopped on the third floor and his stomach caught up, Ribsy heard Larry's frightened voice coming up the elevator shaft from the first floor. "Dog? What dog?" he was saying. "I don't have any dog."

"Don't you lie to me," the manager said. "I know there's a dog in this building."

"It isn't my dog," said Larry.

Upstairs a woman opened the door and pushed back the gate.

"Hello," said the woman to Ribsy, as if she met dogs in elevators every day. "How did you manage to press the button?"

This time Ribsy was taking no chance of being left in this frightening room that made him lose his stomach. He dashed past the woman and into the third-floor hall, while the door of the elevator closed behind him. Now he did not know what to do. He was in a long hall with a strip of worn carpet down the center and doors on either side. At one side of the hall was a staircase, and at the end of the hall was a window with a fire-escape sign over it. Nothing looked familiar to Ribsy, who had never been in an apartment house before.

Larry's voice came up the stairwell. "But I don't *have* a dog."

Ribsy did the only thing he could think of. He started down the stairs toward Larry's voice.

"Young man," said Mrs. Kreech, "you took a dog into that elevator. You can't fool me."

Ribsy hesitated. He did not like this woman's voice. It reminded him of too many voices that had yelled, "You get off my lawn!" to him. Some-

times voices like this were accompanied by a rock or a clod of dirt.

Ribsy heard the elevator door open down on the first floor and the manager say in quite a different voice, "Oh, good morning, Mrs. Berg. I was looking for a dog in the elevator."

"There's no dog in the elevator," said Mrs. Berg, who was a friend of Larry's and who understood the situation. "I have come to pay my rent."

"Certainly," said the manager. "Just step into my apartment while I write your receipt."

Ribsy stood listening at the steps, but all he heard was the elevator door close and the machinery whir. As the elevator rose, Ribsy started cautiously down the steps. He did not know what to expect in this strange building where rooms went up in the air. The second floor looked exactly like the third, which Ribsy had just left—the same strip of carpet, the same doors on either side, the same window with a sign over it at the end of the hall.

Ribsy felt confused. He was even more confused when he heard a whispered, "P-s-s-t!" It was Larry, who was supposed to be down below but who was now up above. While Ribsy had walked down to the second floor Larry had ridden up to the third.

"Wuf!" answered Ribsy, who wanted to get out of this place.

"Sh-h-h!" Larry's worried face appeared in the stairwell above Ribsy. He came tiptoeing down the steps. "I've got to get you out of here," he whispered. "Come on." He started to lead Ribsy on down the steps, when the door of the manager's apartment opened on the first floor.

"Thank you, Mrs. Berg," the manager was saying.

"We can't go down that way," whispered Larry. "Come on, this way."

Ribsy obeyed, because he did not know where to go by himself and because he wanted to stay away from the woman with the angry voice. Larry led him down the hall toward the back stairs, which were near the window with the sign

over it. He was about to start down with Ribsy
when he heard someone coming up.

"I don't know who it is, but I'm not taking any
chances," Larry muttered, looking around wildly.
He saw the window at the end of the hall and
opened it.

Ribsy found himself being picked up, thrust
through the window, and dropped onto the fire
escape. The window was closed behind him and
a curtain pulled. Ribsy's feet slid through the
metal bars of the fire escape and stuck down in
empty space. If an elevator was a strange place,
a fire escape was much, much worse. Ribsy felt
as if he should be falling but, instead, there he
hung in midair. Inside he heard the manager's
angry voice, which made him feel as if he had
done something he should not, but he could not
understand what it was. Silently he struggled to
get all four of his feet up onto the metal bars of
the fire escape.

Ribsy soon discovered that a fire escape was
not only frightening, it was uncomfortable. He

had to move his feet carefully on the cold metal or they would slip through. It made him uneasy to see the ground so far below him. There was an opening in the fire escape big enough to jump through, but the ground was too far down.

Since Ribsy could not go down, he did the next best thing. He went up. Because he was an optimistic dog, he hoped things might be better up there. He climbed up cautiously, one step on the steep slanting ladder at a time. Unfortunately, when he reached the next level of the fire escape, things were worse. The good solid ground was farther away. Ribsy peered into the window, but the third-floor hall was empty.

With his tail drooping, Ribsy looked around. The view was better, but there was nothing a dog would be glad to see—only some old fenders and wrecked cars behind the body-and-fender shop below. He could look out over the roof of the shop and see the cars and buses on the busy street on the other side of the block. He tried whimpering at the window, but no one came. He gave an

experimental bark, but there was so much banging in the body-and-fender shop that no one heard
him.

Bewildered and frightened, Ribsy lay down on
the fire escape as best he could. The cold metal
bars pressed into his body, and the breezes blew
under as well as over him. Nothing was comfortable, nothing was familiar. He felt more lost than
he had ever felt before. There was nothing to do
but lie there on the fire escape, watching the traffic and listening to the banging in the body-and-
fender shop, and wait for things to get better.

A half hour went by and then an hour. Larry
did not come back, and the building was silent,
because the apartments overlooking the body-
and-fender shop were rented to people who were
out all day and did not have to listen to the noise.
Ribsy grew cold and stiff. His body hurt from
the iron bars that pressed into him. Things were
not getting any better. Ribsy would have to do
something.

Ribsy got up and managed to shake himself

without having his feet slip through the fire escape. Cautiously he put one forepaw and then the other on the window ledge once more and whimpered at the empty hall. The doors remained closed. No rescuer appeared. Ribsy became impatient. He barked. Still no one came to rescue him. No one cared about the dog on the fire escape. He was forgotten.

Ribsy turned around carefully and barked through the railing toward the traffic on the next street. The only answer he got was the banging in the body-and-fender shop below. Ribsy walked gingerly around the fire escape to make sure he had not missed a way out. There were only the ladderlike steps, and while he had not minded climbing up, they were much too steep to go down.

Ribsy became frantic. He felt as if the whole world had gone off and left him. He barked and barked and barked. There must be somebody someplace who would come and get him off this thing.

And there was somebody. Somebody way down below on the next street. "Ribsy!" It was Henry Huggins' voice coming from the new station wagon, which was moving along with the rest of the traffic. "Ribsy!" Henry had his head out of the window and was pointing up at the fire escape.

At the sound of the voice he loved Ribsy went wild. He barked until he was hoarse. In his excitement his hind feet slipped through the fire escape. Terrified lest he fall through, he scrambled frantically to regain his footing on the metal bars. When his feet were planted safely once more, there was no sign of Henry anyplace. This terrified Ribsy even more. Henry had gone off and left him again. He barked so hoarsely and so wildly that even the body-and-fender men heard him.

One of them came to the back door of the shop and looked up at the dog on the fire escape. "Well, I'll be doggoned," he said, pushing his greasy cap back on his head. "How did you get up there?"

Ribsy whimpered anxiously. He felt better, just having someone speak to him.

"Hey, Bert," the body-and-fender man called to someone in his shop. "There's a dog on the fire escape."

"No kidding?" Bert appeared and looked up at Ribsy. "Well, what do you know? How do you suppose he got up there?"

Ribsy tried to tell the men that he had to get down, that he had to run down the street and find Henry Huggins before he got so far away he could never find him again.

"What do you think we should do?" asked the body-and-fender man.

Bert shrugged. "Probably some kid put him there. Most likely it was Larry. He'll probably get him down again."

"Yeah. I guess you're right." The two men knew Larry, who often came into the shop to admire the wrecked cars.

Suddenly Ribsy saw Henry Huggins appear from around the side of the building. "Ribsy!" the boy shouted. "I've found you!"

This time Ribsy barked for joy at the sight of the boy down below.

"Funny place to lose a dog," remarked the body-and-fender man.

"I didn't lose him there," explained Henry, his eyes on his dog. "I lost him a month ago at the shopping center."

"Then what's he doing up there?" the man asked.

"Search me," said Henry. All that really mattered was that he had found his dog at last. "All I know is I was talking to him on the telephone, and he started running, and nobody saw him after that."

The two men looked at one another, shook their heads, and turned to go back into the shop. One of them said something that sounded like, "Poor kid. Too much TV."

The other said, "Yeah. My boy watches those talking-animal programs too, but he's too smart to believe them."

Next Ribsy saw Henry's mother and father

come around the corner of the apartment house. "I finally found a parking space," remarked Mr. Huggins, and looked up at Ribsy. "Hello there, fellow."

Ribsy made eager, anxious noises. Surely his family would not go off and leave him here.

"See, Dad," said Henry. "I told you if we just drove around in this neighborhood we were sure to find him. I told you he couldn't be too far from that Joe's house."

"You were right, Henry," said his mother. "And now we don't have to argue with that boy Joe about who owns him. How on earth do you suppose he got up there?"

Ribsy whimpered again, to remind Henry he would like to get off this thing.

"What worries me is how we are going to get him down," said Henry.

By this time Larry Biggerstaff arrived. He had been sitting on the front steps worrying about how he was going to get rid of the dog, when he had noticed three people hurry down the side of his apartment building, and had overheard the words "dog" and "fire escape."

"That's easy," Mr. Huggins was saying. "I'll just go ring the bell and tell the manager we want our dog back."

"Please don't do that," begged Larry, bursting into the conversation. "The dog isn't supposed to be there, and I'll catch it if the manager finds out about him. She might even evict me and my mother, like she always says she's going to."

Ribsy barked to remind the people below that he was still up here.

"Sh-h-h," hissed Larry.

"I don't get it," said Henry. "What's he doing up there?"

"Well, I was playing out in front with this old tennis ball I have." From the way Larry spoke of the tennis ball it was easy to tell he did not think much of it. "This dog came along and wanted to chase it. And, well, I got to thinking he might be hungry, and so I started to take him inside, and the manager started chasing me, and

I shoved him out on the fire escape to hide him. And, well, I have been sitting out on the front steps trying to figure out how I was going to get rid of him without the manager seeing me."

"I see," said Mr. Huggins.

"Well, you just get him down," said Henry. "Fast."

"Now, Henry," said his mother.

"I didn't put him out on the third floor," said Larry, as if this helped the situation. "I put him out on the second, and he climbed up to the third."

Ribsy was so eager to get down he put a paw on the ladderlike steps. He could not do it. They were too steep. He was afraid.

"We seem to have a problem," said Mr. Huggins, looking up at the dog on the fire escape.

"Maybe you could boost me up to that little ladder that sticks down from the bottom part, and then I could climb up and carry him down, offered Larry, who was glad someone had arrived to help him with his problem.

"Oh, no," said Mrs. Huggins hastily. "We

couldn't let you climb down those steep steps with a dog. You might slip."

Ribsy could not be patient any longer. He put his paw on the top step again.

"Maybe we could call the fire department and they could bring a net and he could jump," suggested Henry.

"Don't do that! Please don't do that." Larry objected strenuously. "The manager really gets excited when she sees a fire engine in front of the building."

Ribsy was beginning to think the people below had forgotten all about him. He put a second paw on the steps. He wanted so much to get down. He wanted to feel Henry petting him again and to lick his face. Even though he was afraid, he was going to try.

"This is ridiculous," said Mr. Huggins. "I'll just go in the back door and up the back stairs and bring him in through the window."

"And have someone mistake you for a burglar?" asked Mrs. Huggins. "Oh, no!"

"You go," Henry said to Larry. "You got him up there."

Larry looked frightened. "The manager might catch me."

"Then I'll go," said Henry.

Ribsy reached for the second step and at the same time brought his hind feet down to the top step.

"No, you won't," said Henry's mother. "You can't go roaming around in a strange building."

"We can't just leave him—" Henry began.

Ribsy had started down the steep steps. It was too late to turn back even if he wanted to, and he did not want to. He found himself coming down the steps faster than he expected. The metal was slippery to his paws. Halfway down he slipped and tumbled, yelping, to the bottom, and there he was with his feet dangling in space again.

"Hey, look!" Henry pointed unnecessarily. Everyone was looking at Ribsy. "He got down by himself! That proves he wants to come home to us."

Ribsy picked himself up and scrambled around trying to find places to set his feet.

"Did you hurt yourself, Ribsy?" Henry asked.

Ribsy managed to set his feet on the slats of the fire escape. "Wuf!" he said, and wagged his tail to show that he was still all right.

"Smart dog, Ribsy!" said Henry. "Now how do we get him down from there?"

The two men from the body-and-fender shop came out once more to see what all the commotion was about. "I hear that dog talks on the telephone," remarked Bert.

"He did once," said Mr. Huggins absentmindedly. He was wondering how they were going to get Ribsy down to the ground.

The two men exchanged a glance. "There's a ladder in the shop that should reach almost to the bottom of the fire escape," one of them said. "I'll get it." He returned in a moment with a paint-spattered stepladder, which he set up under the fire escape. It almost reached the metal ladder that extended down from the fire escape.

"I'll go, Dad," said Henry, eager to get his hands on his dog again.

"You'd better let me go," said his father, mounting the stepladder.

With help so near, Ribsy barked joyfully.

"Sh-h-h!" hissed Larry.

Mr. Huggins climbed the stepladder and then the short ladder that was part of the fire escape. He crawled through the opening in the lower level of the fire escape and picked up Ribsy. "Hold still, boy," he said, as Ribsy gratefully tried to lick his face.

"You'll fall," worried Mrs. Huggins. "You can't possibly climb down the fire-escape ladder and the stepladder with a dog."

"Don't drop him," begged Henry.

"I'm afraid that's what I will have to do," said Mr. Huggins.

"Go ahead," said one of the body-and-fender men. "We'll catch him."

Ribsy felt himself being lifted over the railing of the fire escape, and then he experienced a terrible moment of panic as he fell through the air. Suddenly everything was all right. Four strong hands caught him. Ribsy wriggled out of the grasp of the body-and-fender men and sprang into Henry's arms, where he licked Henry's face for joy.

"Ribsy!" said Henry. "Ribsy, old boy!" He put the dog down at last, and Ribsy was so happy he waggled all over. Henry sank to his knees and hugged his dog.

"Whew! That's a relief," said Larry.

Mr. Huggins reached into his pocket and brought out his wallet. "I think part of the reward money should be yours," he said to Larry.

"What for?" Larry looked suspiciously at Henry's father as if he thought he might be joking. "I didn't do nothing."

"You put him up where we could see him," said Mr. Huggins, and held out three one-dollar bills. "If you hadn't put him up on the fire escape, we could have driven around all day without seeing him." Larry looked doubtfully at the bills.

"Sure," said Henry. "You put him up there in plain sight."

Larry took the three bills. "Thanks. I can buy a good ball with this." He grinned at Mr. Huggins and at Henry. Then he patted Ribsy.

Ribsy was so happy he wriggled all over for Larry, too.

"And now I think we'd better go home before Larry's manager catches us," said Mr. Huggins, as the men took down the ladder and carried it into the body-and-fender shop.

"I wonder if that dog knows how to dial the telephone, too," remarked Bert.

"If he does he ought to be on TV," answered the other man.

Henry, his parents, and Larry walked along the side of the apartment house with Ribsy bounding along beside them. In front of the building they ran right into Mrs. Kreech, who was sweeping the front steps.

"I knew you had a dog, Larry Biggerstaff," she said triumphantly. "Wait till I talk to your mother about this!"

"There must be some mistake," said Mr. Huggins politely. "This is our dog. He never belonged to Larry."

"But—" began Mrs. Kreech.

"No," said Mr. Huggins firmly. "The dog is ours, and has been for several years. We just—misplaced him for a while."

Mrs. Kreech did not know what to say, so she went back to sweeping the steps.

Henry opened the door of the station wagon, which still smelled like a new car. "Hop in," he said to Ribsy.

Ribsy accepted the invitation. He jumped in and settled himself on the seat. This time he knew he was welcome. Henry climbed in beside him. He picked up the leather collar, which was lying on the seat, and fastened it around Ribsy's neck. Ribsy thumped his tail on the upholstery.

Mrs. Huggins smiled at Ribsy and did not say a word. Ribsy could ride in the new station wagon all he wanted.